OSCAR BRENIFIER   VIKTORIA CHERNENKO

Philosophizing

with

Zhuangzi

BOOK II

Illustrations by
Sandrine Thevenet

Alcofribas Publisher

Introduction

Most likely, Zhuangzi really existed, but we do not know much about him. He seems to have lived during the fourth century B.C. and can be thought of as the most creative of all early Chinese thinkers. His peculiar style and surprising content grant him a special place in classical literature. He holds a very peculiar function and status within his home culture. For one, he is a "must", an obligation, an essential and unavoidable author in the tradition of Chinese literature and philosophy. But most of his modern compatriots don't read him, or have not read him since school, and really don't know what he stands for, beside sometimes some vague, reductionist or distorted idea. The Zhuangzi is composed of many surprising little stories, written in order to make the reader think. Most Chinese cannot even recall one, although a few of them sound familiar to their ears when they are repeated to them, like the one of the butterfly, or the fishes in the pond. Second, the ideas of Zhuangzi, his modality of thinking, his critical and provocative side, do not correspond to the mental map, to the intellectual manners or routine of most Chinese people. Here, one has to understand that the most important battle of ideas in the history of Chinese philosophy takes place in the opposition between Confucian thinking and Taoist thinking, of which Zhuangzi and Laozi are the main representatives. We put aside Buddhist philosophy, which plays an important role as well, but is not of Chinese origin, even though the Chinese have stamped their mark on this Indian import. As well, we will not enter a scholarly debate about the unity or not of Taoist thinking, the main point being that within the unity of the Chinese philosophical matrix, there is a fundamental fracture, loaded with numerous ideological implications.

When we look at the common way that guides the actions and thoughts of contemporary Chinese citizens, we can observe that Confucianism is rather hegemonic, consciously or unconsciously so. We could make an analogy in the West, where in the original opposition represented by Socrates and Plato on one side, Aristotle on the other side, Aristotle has rather won the historical battle of ideas, since our common worldview is inclined toward a material reality more than toward a reality of ideas. The relation is quite similar in the Confucian/Taoist opposition, although we would characterize it as the opposition between humanistic and idealistic views. Let us take a couple of examples. First, the relation to the Dao, which is the most fundamental common concept within Chinese philosophy, the way "Being" or "God" would be two fundamental or founding common concepts within Western culture. For the Daoist thinkers, the Dao is not a "name" for a "thing" but the underlying natural order of the Universe, whose ultimate essence is difficult to circumscribe due to it being non-conceptual, yet evident in one's being, one's life. It is "eternally nameless" and must be distinguished from the countless 'named' things which are considered to be its manifestations. It is the reality of life, before any concrete example we could describe. But for the Confucians, the term Dao rather indicates the "Truth", or the "Way", as it defines a particular approach to life, to politics and to the tradition. It is a "humanistic" Dao, regarded as necessary in relation to our morality and our humanity. Confucius rarely speaks of the "T'ien Dao" (Way of

Heaven). An influential early Confucian, Hsiin Tzu, explicitly noted this contrast. Though he acknowledged the existence and celestial importance of the Way of Heaven, he insisted that the Dao principally concerns human affairs.

The second example derives from the first: it bears on the criteria for determining and judging our actions. For Confucians, rituals are fundamental: customs and traditions have to be respected. They represent the crucial ordering of society, an important factor of harmony within society, regulating our lowly and individualistic instincts, a regulation which of course has moral connotations. Within this framework, hierarchy is crucial, since it determines the place of each individual in the structure of this harmony. For Taoists, those rituals are at best superficial, at worst an illusion or hypocrisy, since the only principle that has to be referred to and obeyed is the Dao, the cosmic principle. This of course leaves much space for individuality and represents a strong criticism of society, its rules and obligations. This is one of the reasons why Taoists are often perceived as rebels, anarchists or antisocial. Even moral rules are criticized, as a lower level of ethics, below the Dao, the De (power) and benevolence, in a declining order: then comes morality, and lastly the rituals. Confirming the Confucian tendency of Chinese society, one will often notice that when a contemporary Chinese knows a Zhuangzi story and gives his understanding of it, it is often twisted in a moralistic sense, an interpretation which is far from the original preoccupation. The case of the De, which we will deal with later on in our work, often translated as a virtue in a human moral sense, is a good example of this, when it originally means "virtue" in an ontological sense, like in English we would say the "virtue" of a medicine, referring to the useful effects it can have, its efficiency or its power.

Of course, the two traditions sometimes share similar ideas about man, society, the ruler, heaven, and the universe, ideas that were not created by either school but that stem from a tradition prior to either Confucius or Laozi. The latter is generally thought of as founder of philosophical Taoism, which should be distinguished from religious Taoism, a latter invention. But Confucianism limited its field of interest to the creation of a moral and political system that fashioned society and the Chinese empire; whereas Daoism, inside the same worldview, represented more personal and metaphysical preoccupations. Although within this framework, Zhuangzi holds a particular singular, critical and even sarcastic perspective and style, which can be compared to the Greek cynics, like Diogenes, called "a Socrates that went mad". Unlike Confucians, Daoism never had a unified political theory. While Huang-Lao, a latter Taoist, justified a strong emperor as the legitimate ruler, the "primitivists" (like Zhuangzi) argued strongly for a radical anarchism, political life and hierarchy being presented with disdain. One should not be surprised that throughout many dynasties, Confucianism was established as official doctrine by emperors, when Daoism was often barely tolerated or even banned as a doctrine.

But there is another aspect of Zhuangzi which is even more provocative for Chinese contemporaries: it is quite contrary to the values commonly promoted within society and the family. First of all, what can be called ambition and greed, with its relation to success and hard work, established as crucial moral values, including competition and the struggle for survival. Those values, the worldview they represent, is today quite widespread and strongly so. One has to make it! Be it by trying to pass the indispensable Gaokao (a demanding university entrance examination), by ranking at the top of the class, by climbing the social ladder, by becoming rich and recognized, by wanting to be respected and not lose face, the ordinary Chinese citizen is totally at odds with the Zhuangzi principles. Although one can claim as well that in the west most people are at odds with the idealistic perspective of most philosophers. Therefore, in spite of the admiration Zhuangzi suscitates as a great and famous thinker, he is easily viewed in a reductionist way as someone who promotes "doing nothing" and "life outside of society", a behavior which of course is considered impossible, idealistic and unrealistic. A sort of common wisdom half-jokingly states that Confucianism is for young and working people, Taoism is for retired people, who have nothing to accomplish anymore. Lastly, we encounter the criticism of family values that often provides a feeling of goodness in the conscience of the Chinese citizen. Zhuangzi invites us to escape this illusory, selfish, reduced and limited perspective, and to place ourselves in a much wider perspective, what he calls sometimes the "great ocean", instead of the little pond where small people live in, pretending to be happy, good and safe.

Presentation of Zhuangzi by Robert Eno (Abridged by O.B.)

The literary style of the Zhuangzi is unique, and one needs to adapt to the style and format of the text in order to get into it. Most of the chapters are a series of brief but rambling essays, which mix together statements that may be true with others that are absurd, and tales about real or imaginary figures. It is never a good idea to assume that when Zhuangzi states something as fact that he believes it to be true, or that he cares whether we believe it or not. He makes up facts all the time. It is also best to assume that every tale told in the Zhuangzi is fictional, that Zhuangzi knew that he had invented it, and that he did not expect anyone to believe his stories. Every tale and story in the Zhuangzi has a philosophical point, and those points are the important elements of Zhuangzi's book. The world in which the events of the Zhuangzi occur is not the world in which we live. He tells us about a ten-thousand mile long bird, adding what a cicada and a dove have to say about it. We enter a world filled with fabulous beasts, imaginary plants, and flying immortals. The human population of Zhuangzi's world is unusual as well. His society is filled with sorcerers, hunchbacks, and mysterious hermits, talking rivers, swimmers who can dive down steep waterfalls without fear, and a butcher who carves up ox carcasses with utmost dexterity. One interesting aspects of the Zhuangzi is that one of its chief characters is Confucius. Sometimes Confucius is pictured as a buffoon, a pompous fool despised by characters in tune with Daoist ideas. But frequently Confucius acts as well as a spokesman for Zhuangzi's point of view, and we are left to wonder whether this is just Zhuangzi's way of taunting his Confucian intellectual adversaries or whether he did not, in fact, feel that his ideas shared certain features with those of Confucius.

Zhuangzi's chief strategy is to undermine our ordinary notions of truth and value by claiming a very radical form of fact and value relativity. For Zhuangzi, as for Laozi, all values that humans hold dear – good and bad; beauty and ugliness – are non-natural and do not really exist outside of our very arbitrary prejudices. But Zhuangzi goes farther. He attacks our belief that there are any firm facts in the world. According to Zhuangzi, the cosmos is in itself an undivided whole, a single thing without division of which we are a part. The only true "fact" is the dynamic action of this cosmic system as a whole. Once, in the distant past, human beings saw the world as a whole and themselves as a part of this whole, without any division between themselves and the surrounding context of Nature. But since the invention of words and language, human beings have come to use language to say things about the world, and this has had the effect of cutting up the world in our eyes. When humans invent a name, suddenly the thing named appears to stand apart from the rest of the world, distinguished by the contours of its name definition. In time, our perception of the world has degenerate from a holistic grasping of it as a single system, to a perception of a space filled with individual items, each having a name. Every time we use language and assert something about the world, we reinforce this erroneous picture of the world. We call this approach "relativism" because Zhuangzi's basic claim is that what we take to be facts are only facts in relation to our distorted view of the world, and what we take to be good or bad things only appear to have positive and negative value because our mistaken beliefs lead us into arbitrary prejudices. The dynamic operation of the world-system as a whole is the Dao. The partition of the world into separate things is the outcome of non-natural, human language-based thinking. Zhuangzi believed that what we needed to do was learn how to bypass the illusory divided world that we have come to "see before our eyes," but which does not exist, and recapture the unitary view of the universe of the Dao. Like Laozi, Zhuangzi does not detail any single practical path that can lead us to achieve so dramatic a change in perspective. But his book is filled with stories of people who seem to have made this shift, and some of these models offer interesting possibilities, such as Cook Ting or the Wheelwright. These exemplars seem to have found a way to re-perceive experience through the mastery of certain types of skill, and this may be one route that Zhuangzi is suggesting to guide us towards the new world perspective that escapes the prison that language has built for us. In another section, Zhuangzi has Confucius formulate the following regimen, called "the fasting of the mind," for his disciple Yan Hui: Make your will one. Don't listen with your ears, listen with your mind. No, don't listen with your mind, listen with your qi. Listening stops with the ears, the mind stops with recognition, but qi is empty and waits on all things. The Dao gathers in emptiness alone. Emptiness is the fasting of the mind. Confucius's description seems to suggest some form of meditation practice, but the results look similar to the outcome of Cook Ding's more athletic performance of ox-carving.

These portraits of ways towards wisdom suggest that while Zhuangzi believes that our ideas about facts in the world are fundamentally distorted forms of knowledge, he does not hold a completely relativistic view of knowledge. Cook Ding and Zhuangzi's Confucius do seem to have reached some level of wisdom, but their knowledge seems to be of a very different kind from the knowledge people more ordinarily prize. There is no single Zhuangzi syllabus that can compare to the elaborate ritual syllabus that Confucius devised for his school. But Zhuangzi does seem different from Laozi in trying to give concrete hints about the path to his vision of perfected wisdom.

The pleasure of fishes

Zhuangzi and Huizi were wandering on a bridge above a moat when Zhuangzi said: "See how the minnows come out and dart around where they please! That's what fishes really enjoy!" Huizi said, "You're not a fish. How do you know what fishes enjoy?" Zhuangzi said, "You're not me, so how do you know I don't know what fishes enjoy?" Huizi said, "I'm not you, so I certainly don't know what you know. On the other hand, you're certainly not a fish. So that still proves you don't know what fishes enjoy!" Zhuangzi said, "Let's go back to your original question, please. You asked me how I know what fishes enjoy —so you already knew I knew it when you asked the question. I know it because I'm standing above the moat."

Relativism

Relativism designates the doctrine or belief that a given truth is not universally valid, and it should be evaluated only in relation to different parameters, within a given context. It presupposes that views are relative to differences in perception, sentiments, and intellectual paradigms. Any judgment is produced and determined within given conditions, such as personal situation, limits of language, cultural schemes, etc. As a logical consequence, one can conclude that there is no such a thing as a universal, objective truth, since each point of view has its own truth, its own legitimacy. Different types of relativism vary in their degree of scope and their intensity. It can affect primarily moral issues –determination of good and bad as a guide to our actions, and cognitive issues–determination of truehoods and falsehoods to judge knowledge propositions. Relativism in general tries to avert different types of projections, such as ethnocentrism: the fact of judging other cultures by the standards of our own culture. Social constructivism nevertheless establishes that judgments and norms can be evaluated within the context of a given culture. The main point of a contemporary form of relativism called postmodernism is the refusal of what is called "great narrations": such a criticism of "truth" is justified by the argument that what is considered "true" is not based on logical or empirical data, as is often believed and claimed, but relies on "accepted stories", the social conventions underlying our knowledge of the world. Such perspectives will oppose the principle of anthropological invariants, since no human values or criteria can be considered absolute. Different brands of relativism have been encountered since very early times, such as in Greek antiquity, often to denounce any transcendental perspective, both from an ontological standpoint – some objective grounding of reality, and from an epistemological standpoint–fixed modalities of knowledge. Plato quoting the sophist Protagoras as saying "Man is the measure of all things", is a famous example of some ancient relativistic thinking, since the way we "perceive" anything would determine its "reality".

An important concept of postmodernism should be mentioned in this context: deconstruction, initially proposed by Martin Heidegger and developed by Jacques Derrida. Its basic criticism of classical western philosophy is that is presupposes and favours the principle of logos, reason, and the idea of presence, the existence of a sort of shadowy and absent author, which all together implies some coherency, some transcendent unity to any speech, a type of "logocentrism" which is considered abusive. Its fundamental intellectual posture is one of criticism and mistrust, of freedom and rupture, towards traditional ideologies of modernity, such as humanism. In opposition to such a "dogmatic" world vision, is proposed the idea of "absence" and "trace". Within this paradigm, human culture is considered as a disjointed plurality of "markings" and "signs", with the "absence" of an author. Therefore, one should analyse speech by identifying confusion in meanings, blind spots, omissions, and contradictions, rather than some "unifying principle". In that sense it would unveil the truth of speech though deconstructing the "objectivation" of the content, opening new spaces of meaning. The differences and oppositions thus identified can never be resorbed within the "logos", within rationality or a given concept: they remain as pure pluralities and arbitrary positivity. This given multiplicity is the actual horizon of life and meaning, always scattered.

There are many reasons to criticize relativism. Already from a pure logical standpoint, to state that "Everything is relative" or "There is no absolute truth" is self-contradictory. For if these propositions are taken as true, they must apply to themselves, and they therefore become false, since they at the same time claim and deny universality. Most commonly, the reference to science, with its body of observational and experimental evidence, is used to criticize cognitive relativism. Often, from a materialist perspective, the criteria of favouring/damaging life and well-being, or protecting the environment, is used to criticize moral relativism. Religious doctrine, with its emphasis on specifying good/bad behaviour from the standpoint of revelation is another important angle of attack, just as customs and tradition. Lastly, relativism can be criticized as a form or lazy or complacent thinking, a very common attitude, where "everything depends", without any idea of the nature of this dependency, a vague theorization about the complexity of knowledge, prohibiting any judgment, paralyzing any advancement of the thinking.

In the present situation, both Zhuangzi and Huizi can indeed observe the swimming around of the minnows in the water "the minnows come out and dart around", and no debate or controversy takes place around those observations, taken as empirical data, for right or wrong. But when Zhuangzi makes assertions about the "feelings" of the fishes, about their motivations and their pleasure, "where they please! That's what fishes really enjoy!"; Huizi intervenes and denies him the legitimate right to formulate such a statement. Not just that he should not say it, but that he should not even think it, since such a judgment has for him no foundation. Such a judgment is what Kant would call a "synthetic judgment", since it is not simply based on empirical observation or data, but is constructed with the help of general knowledge and reasoning, that the mind deems to apply to a given phenomenon, object or situation. One could say, independently of the value we attribute to the words of Zhuangzi that he is speculating, and that is precisely on this issue that Huizi objects, viewing this speculation as "mere" or "empty" speculation. One can see that the fishes "move around", but one cannot see the "enjoyment": this judgment is a cognitive leap produced by associating an empirical observation with some reasoning and knowledge about reality as we know it.

Of course, many a reader will tend to support the position of Zhuangzi against such "unfair" criticism, since what he says seems to fit our idea of common knowledge or common sense. But let us examine the different angles through which this criticism could make sense or at least be accepted. In this case, we are more interested in the intellectual paradigms which constitute the substance of the dialogue, the stakes this narration exemplifies, than by the reality of "fish happiness" or not. First criticism, rather implicit, is the apparent categorical nature of the statement: Zhuangzi seems to be confident in his own judgment, he speaks as if he knew with certainty what is happening, since nothing in his words indicates any doubt or element of subjectivity. Second criticism is the accusation of anthropocentrism: Zhuangzi is not a fish, he is a human, therefore he can only project his humanity, his human functioning, his human bias on the fishes, which makes no sense since those animals are endowed with a totally different nature. Huizi accepts the idea of enjoyment, which he could as well reject, but he denies to Zhuangzi the possibility of identifying the object of this enjoyment in the fishes. He asks, "How do you know what fishes enjoy?", but it is a rhetorical question: it means, "you don' t know what fishes enjoy", and furthermore "you cannot know what fishes enjoy".

Zhuangzi, always playful, decides to "judo" this argument, by taking this "logic" all the way, using it against his author. "You're not me, so how do you know I don't know what fishes enjoy?" In other words, he pushes relativism further, claiming that in the same way that "Zhuangzi cannot know what fishes enjoy since he is not a fish, therefore Huizi cannot know what Zhuangzi knows since he is not Zhuangzi. To insist on the irony of the response, the latter takes up the same form of speech as his counterpart: a rhetorical question.

At this point, we should say a few words about Huizi, who periodically appears in the Zhuangzi, as his favourite intellectual interlocutor. He was a statesman and a philosopher, who lived during the Warring States Period, roughly between 380−305 B.C. A major representative of the important "School of Names", he could be called a sophist, in the sense given to this term by Plato. It refers to knowledgeable men, often teachers, specializing in the usage of philosophy and rhetoric, who had a vast knowledge of culture. Plato opposed the sophist to the philosopher, since the latter is searching for truth and wisdom, when the former already holds the truth and wisdom, and mainly wants to prove that he is right. One could say the difference of attitude is crucial in this matter. Since the sophist practices "eristics": he wants to argue in order to prove his point, when the philosopher prefers "dialectics" to examine ideas in order to investigate the nature of thought and knowledge. For example, Huizi enjoyed producing paradoxes about the relativity of time and space, holding a rather sceptic and relativist perspective that we can observe in the present text. The narration describes him as picky on logic and language, but not able to capture the profound truth of Zhuangzi, who offers a sort of communion with the world. His formal approach to thinking does not allow him either to understand the playful and humorous dimension of his interlocutor. He focalizes on details, he is unfocused, he gets lost in his mental tricks and his knowledge, he plays on words in a meaningless way. Although he is presented as rather sympathetic, and probably the best contradictor of Zhuangzi. His function in the text reminds us of the way Socrates uses sophists such as Protagoras and Gorgias in the Plato's dialogues. He acts as an intellectual stimulus, by supporting a critical and alternative position, sometimes humorous, and consciously obnoxious. From there his sceptic or relativistic treatment of the Zhuangzi words.

Visibly, Huizi is forced in a corner by the logical irony of his interlocutor. Thus, in the following reply, even though he admits the logic presented to him, he retreats from his radical relativist position, by formulating a categorical judgment in a rather strong fashion: "you are certainly not a fish". Not only does he state what "reality" is, but he adds the forceful adverb "certainly". The implication here is that after all there is some certainty in our cognitive processes, even in the mind of staunch sceptics. This issue intersects two fundamental ideas of our philosopher. First of all, "the illumination of the obvious", an important concept we will deal with at a later point, which supports such a statement. Second, the "great mutation of beings", a principle which goes against such an evidence of distinction, another interesting concept that we will as well develop later on. But the important philosophical issue at this point is that Zhuangzi demonstrates that the relativist position encounters necessarily its own demise at some point: it is not credible, it cannot sustain itself on the long run. Subjacently, and more generally, we encounter the idea that any paradigm is indeed limited: no established system of idea can exhaust reality, any paradigm contains its own flaws. That is the reason why in the Zhuangzi we encounter many shifts in perspective, although it is not of relativistic nature.

It is sometimes tempting to qualify Zhuangzi as a relativist, if only because of the title of the second chapter: "Discussion on Making All Things Equal". And indeed we see many stories where what seems different is actually equal, like the monkey keeper story, and he does invite us to view indifferently reality from different perspectives which are not hierarchized, since each thing has its own place, its own nature, and each phenomenon has its own value that follows from its own nature, which tend to equalize viewpoints. This has to be viewed mainly as a criticism of the Ruist conception, wherein hierarchy is omnipresent, a view that Zhuangzi perceives as abusive, unjustified and even unjust, for example in the social structure. But there is a problem with taking this reading too literally or too radically. For Zhuangzi would have to therefore acknowledge that his own position is no better than those he appears to critique. He would have to recognize that his Daoist philosophy is no improvement over Confucianism after all, and that it is not less short-sighted than the logic-chopping of the Mohists. This is a consequence that Zhuangzi would not recognize, a simple indication that a radical relativistic interpretation of his work is clearly a misreading.

Perspectivism

Perspectivism is the view that perception, experience, and reason change according to the viewer's relative perspective and interpretation. Therefore, judgment of truth or value is contextually determined. This implies that no way of seeing the world can be taken as certain or definitively "true", but in opposition to relativism, it does not entail that all perspectives are equally valid, as matter of pure subjective choice, or mutually exclusive. It rejects the idea of perspective-free worldview, where our thinking would perfectly fit reality like from the eye of God, or even interpretation-free objective reality. As a consequence, there are no purely objective facts, nor any knowledge of a thing-in-itself. No evaluation can transcend cultural formations or subjective designations. There are no ethical or epistemological absolutes. Rules and principles (philosophical, scientific, etc.) are constantly re-assessed according to the circumstances of specific perspectives. "Truth" is nevertheless possible, thus produced by integrating different vantage points together, although comparing them and confronting them, without any need to eliminate one or the other. Each perspective is taken within its individuated context, and subsumed, adding to the overall objective measure of a proposition under examination.

Perspectivism presents itself as a sort of in-between, or a balanced philosophical solution between rationalism and relativism. Between the truth of rationalism, which is a universal truth but without life, since it is abstract and formal, even dogmatic, and does not really allow for substantial singularities and differences, and the truth of relativism, which is a singular truth, limited in scope, since it only applies to some group or individual. Perspectivism posits that the truth depends on a grounded, valid perspective, established from a particular point of view, but complementary to other points of view. Some of the most famous perspectivist philosophers are Montaigne, Leibniz, Nietzsche, Pascal, and Ortega y Gasset, a classical list to which we will add the name of Plato. Perspectivism qualifies the philosophical doctrines or systems defending the idea that reality consists of the totality of different perspectives we have on the world. In other words, it is the addition and confrontation of different points of view that we have about reality that constitute reality. It rejects the idea that man could have access to an a priori objective and universal reality, regardless of a situation, a cultural context or a subjective appreciation. There are no objective facts in themselves, nor is there knowledge of a thing without the perspective of a knowing subject. Therefore, there is no absolute metaphysical, epistemological or moral foundation, no particular position or paradigm can remain unquestionable and limitless in extent, validity and power. A perspective is in this case not a simple fiction, not an imaginary phantasm, not a mere groundless shallow opinion, but an actual dimension of reality; it is in fact the very organization or structure of reality.

Even though perspectivism has certain definite characteristics, in particular by articulating a multiplicity of perspectives, a composite conception of truth, it can vary in style, nature, or attitude. It can be more or less inclusive, more or less critical and polemic, more or less defending a certain vision of the world or ontology. Montaigne advocates the variation of points of view in space and time, and applies it to the study of "oneself". Blaise Pascal, in his geometry, shows that the same cone, according to the position of the plane where it is projected, gives very different geometrical figures. For the philosophical domain, he writes: "Things are true or false according to the face by which we look at them".

But let us take the example of Leibniz, who enjoys the principle of agreeing with most of the ideas he encounters, adding that most schools of thought "are right in much of what they say, but not so much in what they deny". His ontology is that the universe consists of an infinite number of substances called monads, each monad, irreducible to others, representing the universe in a particular way. Interested in all aspects of human knowledge, he maintained an enormous correspondence with thinkers of his time, tried to reunite the numerous Christian churches (without much success), and attempted to reconcile such different philosophers as Plato, Aristotle, Democritus, Descartes, Locke and others. In opposition to Descartes, who pretended to ignore his predecessors, Leibniz ventured to penetrate the numerous previous doctrines. He saw the first in the history of philosophy a progress, the evolution of an "eternal philosophy" which grows deeper and wider with the unfolding multiplicity of ideas and schools, a perspective that Hegel would eventually inherit. He is also one of the first occidental philosophers interested in Chinese philosophy. He is eclectic rather than syncretic, since he does not try to combine or unite the numerous systems or doctrines: he just attempts to identify their general principles and draw some general conclusions about it, such as his famous "Principle of sufficient reason", often viewed as a major law of classical logic. It states that every phenomenon must have a reason, a cause or ground that can be understood, rejecting the possibility of any brute event, or unexplainable fact.

Such general principles are what protects perspectivism from falling into relativism: the diversity nevertheless follows some principle of orderly variation, avoiding arbitrariness and a causality: it is not scattered. Perspectives can as well be hierarchized according to their extension, their potency, their degree of universality. For example, an ethics that can take into account the "place of others" is more operational than the one taking in account only oneself. In this sense, throughout diversity, a perspectivist thinking always searches as a regulatory ideal for some type of coherence or unity, while remaining conscious that the diversity is actually constitutive of a reality. The unity is always residual, it always escapes. Thus, a given action can be thought simultaneously good and bad, a given proposition true and false, with a common ground. One could say it is dialectical.

In a similar way, we can claim that Plato's works are perspectivist. Not so much because they do not contain any particular doctrine, but because through the very concept of dialogue we encounter a plurality of doctrines. Each one is true within the limits of the argumentative function which presents it and justifies it in a substantial way, within a specific dialogical context. For example, in the Symposium, Plato presents a different conception of love, concluded by the one of Socrates. All the speeches can be considered true, presenting different perspectives –e.g. physical or intellectual–that are in fact not rejected, but rather incorporated by Socrates into a broader perspective. The outlining of the initial theses are sufficiently credible to not be considered illusory or false. We neither come to the conclusion that there is not a "Truth", nor that "Truth" is unique and explicit: we are invited to share the view that we can obtain no more than multiple and partial perspectives onto that "Truth". While there is for Plato only one reality, the principle of perspectivism entails that this unity cannot be captured by any unique and definitive formulation. Each formulation will be conditioned by the circumstances and specific concerns of a particular dialogue, concluding to the irreducible multiplicity of perspectives. There are therefore no ultimate doctrines, but only conclusions relative to the context of a specific dialogue, or more generally a non-conclusion or dead-end, as we observe in many Socratic dialogues.

The problem is not that there are no doctrines in Plato's dialogues, but rather that there are numerous doctrines. All hypotheses are provisional. And the reader will encounter numerous contradictions, for example on the nature of the soul, which is dealt in many different and opposite ways, e.g. if it is one or multiple. Many hypotheses appear in a very ephemeral way, to quickly disappear and be contradicted, which does not make them less interesting or enlightening. This is one of the reasons why we should render full justice to the literary and dramatic character of the dialogues, not falling into the trap of turning them into mere literary games with no positive philosophical content, as a mere ornament of some explicit or hidden moral, where the interlocutor of Socrates is a mere vain character or stupid sidekick. Even if we can identify some preferred philosophical position of the author, the exchange and variations on the theme creates a background, granting necessary depth and meaning to this preferred thesis. Indeed, we can prefer a given angle on a statue or consider one side more meaningful, –e.g. the face more than the side–but the depiction of all the angles allows us to understand and perceive better the reality of the statue, which transcends the totality of these perspectives. The dialogue "Parmenides" is another good example of this, where throughout the process different ontological schemes are examined. The protagonists are two important philosophers, Parmenides and Zeno of Elea, and a young Socrates, examining the issue of the oneness or not of being, the primacy of the "One" or of "Being", all aspects of which will be careful examined, in order to sort of introduce a non-dogmatic perspective of Being, in opposition to the rigid Parmenidean primacy of the "One".

Let us now examine the Zhuangzi, in order to show a similar perspectivism, a rather rare occurrence within the context of Chinese philosophy and cultural tradition. The most striking aspect of such a philosophical attitude is the patchwork nature of this opus. In between short analytical development, we are presented numerous scenes, myths, or, anecdotes of various nature and origin, often of bizarre or uncanny nature. Human beings, animals, allegories, mythical creatures, are populating the text in an apparently non-sequitur way, often esoteric or allusive. This literary form can in fact produce quite a rebarbative and repulsive effect on the reader, who will feel estranged or lost, incapable of giving meaning to the parts and to the whole. But with some patience and distance, one will notice that in order to go through those piecemeal writings, one needs to concentrate on each literary moment and be sufficiently flexible in order to capture the issues presented in each of those strange vignettes. If the reader is looking for a systematic exposition, for an explicit treatise, for a univocal message, he will be troubled, disappointed, or even irritated. The second aspect displaying perspectivism is the dialogue form, often chosen to present an issue. First of all, with many predecessors or other famous intellectuals, for example Huizi in the present story, but as well Laozi, Confucius, Yi'erzi (a Mohist), Xu You (another Daoist) and others, who will engage in diverse dialogues or arguments. Confucius, one of his favorite characters, is presented in many different ways, some of them faithful to the historical figure, some of them betraying him, in a totally eccentric, imaginative or even disrespectful fashion. The main point is not to be formally rigorous, but to make the reader think by surprising him or even shocking him, a real challenge to the extent he suffers from any rigidity. What can be called the performative dimension of speech: to create an impact on the reader, shaking him out of his intellectual routine. All the references to the tradition, be they scholarly elements, tales, or religious beliefs, are very loosely displayed and used. His dialogues involve very different types of characters: rulers, robbers, deformed, or even monstrous persons, teachers, craftsmen, each one representing a particular perspective on reality, although the description of their words and behavior is often far from realistic, or could be described as surrealistic. We are therefore not surprised to encounter as well dialogues or interactions between animals, such as cicada, quail, frog, turtle or dove, or abstract entities, such as shadow, penumbra or chaos.

But when we take for example the story of "Frog and Turtle", the author goes at length to describe both forms of happiness, the "petty" one and the "noble" one, both in a very convincing and credible way. It is only at the end, with a small detail, that he hints at the hierarchy between both forms. The frog is "stunned", indicating that the "petty" way cannot grasp the "noble way". Thus, the Zhuangzi is not deprived of coherence, it is vectorized, there is a unity, there are patterns in this multifarious structure. There is even an ontology, for example the idea of the Dao, a transcendental concept, as exemplified by the "Frog and Turtle" story. But as we know from Laozi, from the initial stanza of the Dao De Jing: "The Dao that can be told of is not the eternal Dao; The name that can be named is not the eternal name. The Nameless is the origin of Heaven and Earth." It would therefore be pointless and impossible to name or explain in any specific way the "Truth" of all things: we can only allude to it. Just like with other perspectivist thinkers, the absolute transcends all words, theories and empirical realities, we can only hint at it, by observing its contradictory and paradoxical traces within the mundane world.

At the same time, Zhuangzi is not a relativist: ideas are not for him a matter of pure subjectivity or simple opinion. He wants his reader to think and enter deeper important ontological, epistemological, and existential issues. As we have evoked, this is probably a major difference between the relativist and a perspectivist. The first mainly describes factual situations, scattered, pure posited events, or arbitrary assertions. The latter, and that is definitely the case here, opens various spaces of meaning though a living multiplicity, but hints or even attempts to evoke some unseizable reality underlying this multiplicity. In Zhuangzi, the Dao plays the same function as the western Logos: there is a universal reason or common principle behind this diversity. We know for example that man escapes the Dao because of his "intentions": what would be called today his subjectivity. Through many metaphors, Zhuangzi invites us to perceive some transcendence, like the "origin" of all things, for example "Hundun": the chaos, characterized as mother "Heaven and Earth", or the infinite dimension of reality, serving as the metric of all that exist, or the infinite series of causal relations, and as well the "great mutation", the process by which everything is transformed, inspired by the "Book of Changes". On the cognitive level, we simultaneously have a permanent dialectical approach, where one idea becomes its contrary, a recurrent invitation to transvaluation —shifting connotations of judgments from positive to negative—, the practice of ambiguity, but as well the "illumination of the obvious", which invites the mind to cease and desist its complicated operations and just accept what is presented to it. All the different scenes and ideas teach and reinforce the experience of those paradoxical principles. In a way to address what can be called the human problem of alternate "Daos".

Wandering

Zhuangzi entitled the first chapter of his works "Hsiao yao yu", which means "Leisurely roaming", "Rambling without a destination" or "Wondering beyond". To wander is to travel aimlessly from place to place. The word xiaoyao means "free, at ease, leisurely, spontaneous", it reflects the attitude of the Daoist who is in spontaneous accord with the natural world, and who has retreated from the anxieties and dangers of social life, in order to live a healthy and peaceful natural life. It conveys the impression of people who have given up the hustle and bustle of worldly existence and have retired to live a leisurely life outside the city, perhaps in the natural setting of the mountains. But as well it can refer to a state of mind, to the inner peace of a person who is not affected by external solicitations, who is not disturbed by the chaos of the world, who – like the wooden rooster – does not allow himself to be hassled by whatever pressure or distractions society imposes on him. The Dao is very much a matter of self-mastery, even more than an actual material situation.

The second word, "yao" means "distance" or "beyond", implying to venture beyond the boundaries of familiarity, escaping repetition and routine. We ordinarily confine ourselves within our social roles, we are determined by our expectations, by our values, by our everyday understanding of things. According to Zhuangzi, this type of behavior is inadequate for a deeper appreciation of the nature of things, for a more successful mode of interacting with them, for a better understanding or reality. We need to free ourselves from preconceptions preventing us from seeing things and events in new ways; we need to see how we can structure and restructure the boundaries of things. But we can only do so when we ourselves have "wandered beyond" the boundaries of the familiar. It is only by freeing our imagination that we can reconceive ourselves and our world, that we may begin to understand the deeper tendencies of the natural transformations by which we are all affected, and of which we are all constituted. By loosening the bonds of our fixed preconceptions, we bring ourselves closer to an attunement to the potent and productive natural way of things, to the Dao. We can connect such an attitude to the "wu wei", the non-action, meaning the action without intention, since the action thenceforth is free and guides itself, since it is not bound and bent on some particular result. The action is then taken for its own sake, its own value and benefit, and not in the reductionist acceptance of a mere means for some result. But it is not just the crossing of horizontal boundaries that is at stake. Often Zhuangzi connects the "roaming" and the "soaring", the horizontal and the vertical. One rises to a height from which formerly important distinctions lose what appeared to be their crucial significance.

Horizontal or vertical, arises the distinction between the great and the small, or the "vast" (da) and the "petty" (xiao). Petty understanding remains confined and defined by its limitations, it cannot match the expansive understanding that wanders beyond. Indeed, the "vast" might lose sight of distinctions noticed by the petty, but it still embraces the "petty" in virtue of its very vastness. The "petty", precisely in virtue of its smallness, is not able to reciprocate. Of course, the "vast" that goes beyond our everyday distinctions also appears to be useless to petty minds. A soaring imagination may be wild and wonderful, but it is extremely impractical and often altogether useless. Thus, in other passages, Huizi chides Zhuangzi for this very reason. Zhuangzi expresses disappointment in him: his inability to sense the use of this kind of uselessness is a kind of blindness of the spirit. The useless has utility, contrary to what is perceived on the ordinary level of practical affairs. It has a use in the cultivation and nurturing of the "shen" (spirit), so that one can live a flourishing life, a notion that is not to be confused with a "successful" life. Although flourishing life may indeed look quite unappealing from a traditional point of view. Since one may give up social ambition and retire in relative poverty to tend to one's "shen" and cultivate one's "xing" (nature, life potency).

In the present story, we are right away plunged into the "Hsiao yao yu", with the words "Zhuangzi and Huizi were strolling along". We cannot avoid noticing the absence of purpose, the calm, a context propitious to casual conversation and meditation. As well, we are next to the river, a landscape that often indicates untroubled and slow meandering, unless specified otherwise. Lastly, the two companions must be contemplating the bottom of the river, since they mention the minnows swimming around, another aspect of the description which confirms to the reader the peacefulness of the whole situation. But this staging is not accidental: as we indicated previously, it is essential to thinking, it constitutes the very condition of possibility of appropriate thinking, the attitude conducive to a clear mind.

Before concluding on this concept, there is a last point we should raise about "wandering", not so visible in the present story, but more visible precisely in the first chapter which is called "Leisurely wandering". In that story, Zhuangzi opposes two "forms" of wandering: the wandering of Peng, the giant bird transformed from a giant fish, who travels very high for a few months, trying to reach the "Southern Oblivion", the "Pool of Heaven", while the cicada, the little dove and the quail "twitter and flutter between the bushes and branches." The latter laugh at the endeavor of Peng, for them such a long trip seems harsh, difficult and totally absurd. They think they are free while Peng is not, since wandering should be an effortless, pleasurable and purposeless journey. "Where does he think he's going?", they say. The author then explains that "A small consciousness cannot keep up with a vast consciousness". Peng is actually not making an effort to fly very high: he is flying very high only because it is precisely his way to fly effortlessly. "He can ride the wind, bearing the blue of heaven on his back, unobstructed on all sides, and make his way south." Flying high appears demanding to the little creatures only because they are enclosed in their own particular understanding of flying. And the aim of Peng at "Southern Oblivion" actually implies a total indetermination in accordance with heavenly principle, while the apparently free wandering of the small birds is actually full of physical constraints and a series of puny purposes. This opposition between "little world" and "big world" is a recurrent preoccupation of Zhuangzi. This is to say that wandering is not simply a natural and free action, but something that has to be acquired, otherwise the "free wandering" is actually not so free. And to come back to the present story on the pleasure of fishes, we could say that if Zhuangzi leisurely strolls, since he is available to what he sees, it is not the case with Huizi, since he carries around his own determination, in particular his desire to quibble about just anything and to act smart. An internal constraint which makes him blind and obsessive, which does not allow him the adequate peace of mind. For Zhuangzi, "truth" is not something to be found, a specific object of reflection to delve into, to be stuck upon, but an ambiance in which to dwell, a state of mind, a contemplation that renders one available. That is the essence of the "leisurely strolling", a very demanding state of mind.

Illumination of the obvious

The first remark of Zhuangzi –"See how the minnows come out and dart around where they please!"–is conditioned by the described context: he is in unison with the scenery, in harmony with life processes. This remark would fall under the category of what he calls "illumination of the obvious". Such a qualification applies to a judgment made about a phenomenon, not presented as an absolute or fundamental truth, but within a context, basing oneself "on the everyday function of each being", as the author explains. It does not pretend to be "right", more than it pretends to be "perceptive", or to be "available". In opposition to such an attitude, Huizi is known as a rhetorician, a squabbler, always ready to engage into logical or semantic disputes, such as the famous Chinese intellectual debate on "hardness" and "whiteness", a debate on essence which "entertained" generations of "intellectuals". He is compulsive and bitter, and his main point in most dialogues with Zhuangzi is to introduce very formal disagreements, prohibiting in a rather superficial way substantial thinking processes, in a kind of compulsive problematization, displaying a sort of smart aleck behavior. Huizi wants at the same time to win the argument and to make his interlocutor impotent. Unlike the Socratic systematic questioning, which in spite of its harshness wants to empower the interlocutor through a "purification" process, Huizi, like all sophists, is rather inclined to reduce to ashes his opponent, therefore exhibiting his own power. He is moved by a strong intention, by a determined aim, by a psychological need to show himself. Zhuangzi enjoys discussion with Huizi, his favorite intellectual foe: he will at the same time grant him perfection, for his rigor, while adding that he "distorted his art by attempting to convey it to others", meaning he was corrupted by his attempt to be heard, concluding that "he ended with the darkness of logical disputations". He will regret his death, ironically saying by his grave that "he lost his material".

In opposition to the anxiety of Huizi, Zhuangzi is playful and distant. He toys around with the argumentation, he mirrors his opponent, makes fun of him. He even transgresses logic, in order to produce new insights, to make us look at reality from fresh and unpredictable standpoints. He enjoys freedom, makes fun of the situation, what can be called emancipation through entertainment. In a way, he is in a way less tense than Socrates, since the latter wants something, he expects answers and truth, at least formally, when the former actually aspires to "nothing": "intention" is precisely the main obstacle to the Dao. He calls his path "transcending perfection and imperfection", or the "glimmer of chaos and doubt". He also names it "walking a double path", which he explains as "bringing all into harmony through assertion and denial, resting on the balance of heaven". In a more clear and conceptual way, less metaphorical, one can use the expression of "provisional truth", as Descartes used it. Such a notion captures for him the idea of a given judgment considered true for all practical purposes, within a given context, for a given purpose, as the best possible choice. For example, let us take the important criteria of "clear and distinct perception", dear to rationalist philosophers. A reliable one, if we may say, but which in no way can pretend to be absolutization. It is a necessary condition for truth, and can momentarily function as such, which will we confidently utilize, although it can at any other moment encounter its demise. This strategy is for Descartes the best way to avoid the trap of the doubt engendered by the "evil genius". Since this "evil Genius" threatens to undermine the veracity of the rule, the author assumes the burden of trying to establish the rule, even temporarily. He proposes clarity and distinctness as an underwriting for a general rule of discovering truth. "This would not be enough to make me certain of the truth of the matter if it could ever turn out that something which I perceived with such clarity and distinctness was false." At worse, the "provisional truth" plays the function of filling the gap in current knowledge, since within such a framework knowledge can be considered to exist in degrees of probability. Thenceforth, limits, imperfection or falsehood do not represent any prohibitive obstacle for the enunciation of any judgment.

We can here remind the reader that the epistemological positioning of Zhuangzi echoes his ontological vision: the Dao emanates from chaos, which implies that chaos has left its mark on the harmony of the world. Therefore the "glimmer of chaos and doubt" is not simply because of the fragility and limitation of our mind, since it is constitutive of reality. A perspective from which one is invited "to ride upon" all the transformations in perfect independence and freedom, wherever they may take one, with trust and self-confidence. This is what allows Zhuangzi to calmly state that "That's what fishes really enjoy!", and when the suspicious Huizi challenges him, he simply ends up concluding: "I know it by standing here beside the river Hao.", a good representation of his "illumination of the obvious", which captures a moment of his "leisurely roaming". At the same time, he is not oversimplifying or being complacent, since he practices his art on Huizi as well, by observing and playing with his "logic" just as much. "Let us go back to your original question, please. You asked me how I know what fishes enjoy –so you already knew that I knew it when you asked the question." In this retort, he takes literally the rhetorical question of Huizi to show him that he himself presupposed in his formulation that Zhuangzi knew very well what fishes enjoy, only asking him to specify the source of his knowledge. Classically for him, he applies the "illumination of the obvious" on speech just as he does it on other types of phenomena. This reminds us of the type of analysis produced by Wittgenstein, what can be called nominalist interpretations, in order to avoid the traps and language so common in philosophical works. Both protagonists play games in this dialogue. But when Huizi is anguished and tries to forbid the formulation of any hypotheses, boringly repeating himself, Zhuangzi remains in peace and insouciance through playing with the arguments, allowing himself to produce ideas.

There is another element of the story that justifies or explains the "illumination of the obvious". Zhuangzi says: "I know it because I am standing above the moat.", since he is on the bridge. Now the basic function of a moat is to protect a fortified settlement against enemies from outside. A moat typically marks and separates inner and outer realms, civilization and wilderness, friend and foe, us and them. It supports the function of walls that enclose and define one space against another. Boundary lines are in general what separates and defines identity: it engenders difference. This difference can refer to the "this" and "that" that opposes ideas and things. And it is exactly what Zhuangzi and Huizi are discussing in this passage. Huizi argues that there is an identity difference between Zhuangzi and the fishes, so he cannot know about their happiness. Because of their distinct identity, they have no connection and no access to each other's feelings and knowledge. Thus, when Zhuangzi is asked how he knows about the joy of the fishes, he responds that he knows it because "he is above the moat", on the bridge. From there, he connects the two oppositional sides and bridges the separation of identities. He stands above and beyond the separation. He watches the fishes from a third perspective that is neither that of Zhuangzi or the fishes but has overcome these differences. It is from this perspective above the moat that he is able to know about the happiness of the fishes. And that perspective, the pivot, the center, represents precisely the Dao. The Dao is what allows the illumination of the evidence, since it is what generates everything and every being, perspective which is beyond difference and identity.

Socrates argues for the sake of truth, Huizi argues for the sake of winning, Nasreddin argues for the sake of laughing, Zhuangzi argues for the sake of nothing. The expression "for the sake of something" signifies there is a purpose, an interest, something we want to achieve or preserve. Therefore, we have a direction, and this direction is what gives meaning to our actions. A meaningless action is an action deprived of any purpose, therefore deprived of any meaning. What makes no sense is what is deprived of any intention. There is something loose about the "no purpose", it becomes a "whatever", a totally unspecified entity. "Doing whatever" implies our action can be anything or everything: it will make no difference. It can neither be appropriate or inappropriate, and therefore it is deprived of interest, deprived of importance, deprived of meaning, since this "whatever" can be replaced by any other "whatever". What happens does not matter, what is done does not matter, since the result will be the same. "Whatever you say", your words are deprived of any interest, it will not affect your listener in any way, it announces indifference.

This indifference is commonplace for Zhuangzi. Indifference to the "this or that", indifference to "this theory or that theory", for he criticizes many useless discussions, many useless standpoints, especially fixed and determined standpoints, established perspectives. Although, from his "no-standpoint standpoint", all "standpoints" are criticized, simply because they are "standpoints". As we see in his texts, he proposes to "meander through the perspectives", the same way one can meander through the countryside, without a specific purpose, not getting stuck on determined paths.

Of course, one could here criticize Zhuangzi for this absence of direction or perspective. The consequence of such an attitude would be that we are then absorbed or stuck in the "hic et nunc", in the immediate of the present situation, since there is nothing else in sight. A very poor and limited horizon, one could claim. But actually, to understand the Daoist shift of paradigm, one has to move up on the metalevel. It is not anymore the direction that matters, the "where we go", the determined meaning or perspective, but the type of "attitude" which is called upon, and its cognitive implications. The absence of determined perspective puts us in a state of availability, since our mind is not occupied, or preoccupied, with a specific goal or orientation. We are then open to the unity of all things, to the origin, the fountain, the formless nature that provides form to all forms, basically what is the Dao.

At this point, it might be useful for the reader to convoke a western philosopher who can echo such a perspective, in order to "banalize" the strangeness of such a perspective, in order to bring it closer to home. Nicholas of Cusa, a German Christian philosopher, mathematician and scientist from the Renaissance period. For him, there were two ways to search for the absolute, a concept which can be thought of in religious terms, but which for him structure and guide our search for truth, what can be called an epistemological perspective. The absolute is for one what is deprived of any limit, any constraint, any reduction, any condition: it is therefore the unity of all things, its cause and principle, the being that allows all being to be, although it might be more appropriate to name it "the non-being" that allows all being to be, namely God, who is his own cause and the cause of all else. But the absolute "appears" for him as well, in a different form, what he calls "the reduction of the reduction", or the "contraction of the contraction". In other words, the absolute can be encountered not only in the highest magnitude, in the infinitely wide and potent, in the unconditional eternity, but as well in the infinitely small, in the most minute, what makes a singularity be a singularity, a sort or "local", "contracted" or "reduced" absolute. There is an irreducible nature in the singular, some irreplaceable reality, a limit for the thinking. This has an echo in the principle called the identity of indiscernibles, as formulated by Leibniz, that states that there cannot be separate objects or entities that have all their properties in common. To suppose two things indiscernible is to suppose the same thing under two names. It refers for example to the fact that no two distinct objects, such as snowflakes or leaves can be exactly alike. In this sense, there is something "absolute" in any entity.

Therefore, in our relationship to the world, each entity evokes or echoes the absolute, each "contracted absolute" is consubstantial to the "non-contracted absolute". We encounter this in Zhuangzi, through the Dao. All that exists has its own Dao, which is of the same nature as the Dao itself. But to access this Dao, we should suspend our pre-established ideas about things, and remain in a state of availability. In this context, we are receptive and prepared for the "illumination of the obvious". Through unlearning, our mind is "clean", it can act like a mirror and perceive reality. No dogma or established pattern can interfere with our perception: we are a "receptacle" for the world. But for this we need to apply what Zhuangzi calls "fasting of the mind". When "the spirit is free from all pre-occupation and so waits for things to appear. Where the proper course is, there is freedom from all pre-occupation; such freedom is the fasting of the mind." And it is from this standpoint that Zhuangzi makes the observation about the enjoyment of fishes. When Huizi on the other side intellectualizes the observation and tells Zhuangzi that he cannot know. Here, Huizi acts as a "true philosopher", who immediately criticizes and problematizes what he sees and hears: he wants to argue right away "You are not a fish –how do you know what fishes enjoy?". He overthinks, or worries too much. At this point, Zhuangzi uses the same system and tells him "You are not I, so how do you know I don't know what fishes enjoy?". Stuck, Huizi then tries to use some "evidence": "On the other hand, you are certainly not a fish". By doing this, he gives up on problematization: he is using "illumination of evidence", without realizing it. Once he has done this, Zhuangzi takes the discussion one level higher, on the general principle: "I know it by standing here beside the Hao." "Being here", right here, is the "secret" to knowing. Being present is to be available, it is being with the Dao, and objectively knowing things.

The singular, the immediate, is the key to the absolute.

Comprehension questions

1. What symbolic value has the bridge over the moat?

2. What distinguishes the two walkers and the fish?

3. What occupies the fish?

4. Can Zhuangzi know what the fish like?

5. What can Huizi know about what Zhuangzi knows?

6. Does Zhuangzi have to be a fish to know what a fish thinks?

7. Why does Huizi contradict Zhuangzi?

8. Why does Zhuangzi return to the original question?

9. How does Huizi think?

10. How does Zhuangzi think?

Reflection questions

1. Does our perception play tricks on us?

2. Why is relativism so popular?

3. Can relativism have a value of absolute?

4. What problem does relativism pose?

5. Can we know what animals think?

6. What does it mean to have a point of view?

7. Can we have several points of view?

8. Is changing our point of view a sign of bad faith?

9. How can we know reality?

10. Can we be really objective?

The butterfly dream

Once Zhou dreamt he was a butterfly, a butterfly fluttering gaily. He enjoyed himself very much and he knew nothing of Zhou. Suddenly, he awoke, and all at once he was Zhou. But he did not know whether Zhou had dreamt about being a butterfly or a butterfly had dreamt about being Zhou. Surely there is a difference between Zhou and a butterfly. This is what we call the transformation of things!

Identity

Unlike animals, who simply are what they are, human beings worry about their identity. Actually, animals are worried about their "integrity", since in general they attempt to preserve their own existence, instinctively. Although periodically we observe that "their integrity" is as well, sometimes rather, the one of their species, of their group – herd, pack, colony, or family, etc. The principle we can observe here, as in general in life, is the perpetuation of being, as biologically inscribed within the organism itself, at least evolved ones, if not all of them. Respiration, nutrition, reproduction, the main characteristics of life being all geared to preserving in some form the integrity of one's specific life form. The term "integrity" comes from the Latin construction "not touched" (in -tangere), meaning intact, whole, from which are derived "entire" or "integral". From this we can derive the idea that "touching it" would be considered a threat, implying that integrity has to do with self – protection, with defense against the menace of the outside, considered unfriendly. From integrity to identity, the passage is simple. The Latin term at its origin is constructed around "idem", meaning "same". From this, identity is the quality of being identical, implying that in spite or throughout differences and variations one undergoings, some characteristics of the self should be maintained in order for the identity to be preserved. For without specific constant characteristics, "self" would be meaningless, since nothing would maintain its unity, and nothing would distinguish a "self" from another "self", nothing could modify it or "touch it": it would be undifferentiated, and hence have no 'identity'. Therefore, identity is defined by the principle of "defined, specific and fixed characteristics". Not forgetting, therefore, the fact that those characteristics should be protected from any alienation from the outside. Identity has in a way to remain pure and eternal, "untouched" in both cases.

The passage from "integrity" to "identity" is nevertheless significant. Integrity, taken literally – not as a moral concept – indicates the actual being, primarily biological. Identity is more cognitive, it is more of a constructed concept, since it bears on the formal description of a being, its characteristics, and not simply the being itself, taken as a monolithic whole. Such a description is so important that the concept of identity provides one of the major laws of classical western logic: the principle of identity. This principle states that a thing cannot be itself and its opposite, a fundamental aspect of cognitive structure. Therefore, each entity must have a set of specific characteristics in order to be a separate entity, and it must conserve those characteristics in order to maintain itself as a separate entity. For if "objects" are not defined in some way, nothing can be said about them, no judgment can be made, they cannot be recognized and their knowledge becomes impossible.

For the human being, identity has two different dimensions: one is ontological, another is psychological/existential, which can be opposed as objective and subjective. Ontologically, it is what we are from an objective standpoint, what can be relatively noticed by outside observers, what is a "given" in our being, innate or acquired. Psychologically, or existentially, it is how we conceive of ourselves, a mixture of objective data and subjective constructions. The latter is constituted as a composition of interpretations, fears and desires, personal and social culture. It is articulated in terms of narration, feelings, relations, actions and explanations, what can be called existence. Of course, since man is a "subjective animal", both dimensions can easily overlap upon the other. But what is important in this matter is that just like the animal tries to protect its integrity, the human will try to protect his identity. With the added feature that for the animal, integrity is rather obvious, although issues like the one of the territory –a sort of extended integrity–tends to already complicate the matter, when in human beings the identity has to be constructed, felt or identified, as a condition to be protected, a rather complex process and interaction.

Now that we established a sort of conceptual frame for the identity, let us move on with Zhuangzi and examine the way he deals with the issue of identity in this text. As usual, he goes against the common way of thinking and behaving. He does so by deconstructing the idea of identity, by taking away the certitude of such a concept. Most of the time, human beings search for what they call an "identity", and when they think they have discovered or established this identity, consciously or not, they will go out of their way to affirm it, to proclaim it loudly, to defend it against threats and criticisms. It is actually one of the reasons why we are so sensitive to foreign judgments: it evokes a certain sense of the fragility of this identity, which largely depends on the social acceptance or recognition of it, in order to solidify or consolidate itself. How does he deconstruct it? First, by denouncing it as a dream, taking away its objective and rational dimension. Second, by telling us we might be quite different or exactly the opposite of what we think or hope we are, since indeed a human being and a butterfly are far from identical. "Surely there is a difference between Zhou and a butterfly", says the text. Third, by alluding to the fact we might be much better off being what we are not, being what we do not think we are, or even being what we do not want to be. For indeed he describes the butterfly as being quite happy to be himself while fluttering around, in opposition to Zhuangzi who as a human only knows how to doubt, how to lament, incurring the pain and anguish of his doubt. Fourth, by displaying the freedom there is in the idea of being what "we are not". For what we are is indeed determined, limited and fixed. The range of the "I" is quite restrictive, quite confining, while the range of the "not I" is wide, unlimited and free. He could have chosen some other animal or plant to "dream about", but he chose a butterfly. And what can a butterfly symbolize? Lightness, in opposition to heaviness. Beauty, in opposition to dullness. Freedom, in opposition to necessity. Ephemeral, in opposition to eternal. The four characteristics avoided or opposed by the butterfly are in this way implicitly criticized, characteristics that are typical of the quest for identity.

HEAVINESS   is the state of mind of persons who are anguished about finding some identity, who are eager to protect their identity. This heaviness burdens their personal and relational life, since they always expect and beg for some reassurance on the part of others who on their side have as well their own preoccupation of identity, a difference of agenda that engenders many misunderstandings and conflicts. They want to be strong, they do not appreciate the fleeting dimension of life, the grace of the fragile. They worry a lot, in opposition to the casual, changing and spright lightness of the butterfly. Consciousness here takes a negative turn, in opposition to a careless, effortless, ease and elegance.

DULLNESS   is the feeling that assails many of our fellowmen, who find the reality and routine of their daily life quite far from their expectations and desire for excitement. That is why many of us look for some form of artificial entertainment, as Blaise Pascal criticized it, in order to avoid the feeling of nothingness boredom entails. Partying, drinking, diverse intoxication, gambling, pursuing wealth, gaining power, flirting, working, forming a family, are so many activities we engage into in order not to face ourselves, even though those diverse activities often do not really fulfil our fundamental existential needs.

BEAUTY   Often as well, beauty is not very present in daily activities and preoccupations, since beauty is not the means for something else, contrary to utility, since it represents its own gratification. Beauty is the harmonious unity of singular and universal, of finite and infinite, and it can be seized in the immediate, not in some ideal representation or construction. Identity is what we are now, and we have to be able to perceive its comeliness, the charming characteristic of what exists, the beauty of existence, simply because it exists.

FREEDOM   Necessity, the diktat of needs, internal or external needs, is what guides most persons in the determination of their daily actions.

Internal needs constitute our desires and fears, compulsive psychological obligations that impose themselves on us, since we do not choose to be this way. In fact, if we could freely determine our own life and deliberately elect our desires and fears, it is most likely that many of them would be eliminated. In general, "we do not want our wants", as Leibniz identified it, showing our lack of freedom and the poor appreciation of ourselves. And this applies as well to our fears, and to the different "sad emotions", such as shame, guilt, regret, jealousy, envy, etc. External needs are social obligations, moral diktats, codified rituals, pressure of success, quest for good appearance, etc. In opposition to this, beauty is graceful, unbounded, creative, it points toward transcendence and infinite in the human mind.

EPHEMERAL   The criticism of eternity that represents the ephemeral, in opposition to eternal, is a more subtle and paradoxical issue. The basic idea is that the human heart is lodged in a deep fear of death, of disappearance. Longevity is explicitly one of the main values in Chinese culture, along with wealth and success, all of which can represent a form of social obligation or accomplishment. The omnipresence of the statues of Fu (wealth), Lu (success), and Shou (longevity) in Chinese homes and public places, three gods of traditional religion, are the physical manifestation of this reverence. Fear of death, the anguish about an uncertain future, even if it often provides a drive for accomplishment and existential motivation, represents one of the main sources of dread and worry for many of us. In opposition to this, the butterfly, which lives a very short time, but enjoys each moment of it, without worrying, represents a form of wisdom. Zhuangzi insists on the matter: "a butterfly fluttering gaily. It enjoyed itself very much and it knew nothing of Zhou (Zhuangzi)". The butterfly is enjoying itself, an enjoyment which is visibly related to ignoring Zhou, which can be interpreted as ignoring both humanity and identity, since it neither knows "man" nor "butterfly": it just lives the moment. In Chinese culture, the butterfly symbolizes a beautiful, feminine, delicate, fantasizing nature, the whole opposite of the "speculating" heavy Zhuangzi. The "illumination of the obvious", as we have seen it, a cognitive perspective, has a correspondence on the existential level, as a sort of "carpe diem". Seizing the passing moment, enjoying it and taking advantage of it, is the wisdom of the butterfly, fluttering hither and thither. Not a common human personality, for whom such an "inconsistent" conduct describes either the behavior of a fool, or an extremely wise person.

Mise en abyme

Shadowy, and occluded by the confusion of its supporting theories, the "mise en abyme", for which there is not even an adequate English translation, remains often arcane and obscure, esoteric and elusive. Let us try to simplify it. The "mise en abyme" is a pictorial and literary technique that has its origin in heraldry, the art of armorial bearings. In this domain, the "mise en abyme" describes a coat of arms that appears as a smaller shield in the center of a larger one, both of exact identical shape. It literally signifies "Put in the abyss", where "abyss" – meaning bottomless – designates the center of the shield; in pictorial perspective, what is called "vanishing point". This "mise en abyme" creates a strange effect, eternally recursive, since the larger shield is reflected in the smaller shield, and the smaller shield is reflected in a still smaller shield, a process that can go on indefinitely, reminding us of the matryoshka –those famous Russian dolls that contain themselves through a process of reduction. From there, the "mise en abyme" became a painting technique, popular in the Renaissance, where the painting was represented in the painting, or the painter painting the painting represented in the painting, as it was taken up later on in a famous cereals packaging: we can see on the old packet of Quaker Oats the picture of a man holding a Quaker Oats packet. As well as in literature, where it refers to the technique of inserting a story within a story, the "inner story" evoking or imitating the "outer story", as Shakespeare does in Hamlet for example. Post-modern literature used it as a way of disrupting the continuous logic of the narrative. In philosophy, "abyss" is often a metaphor employed to signify depth without limit, the obscurity of a founding principle, God, Being or else. The "mise en abyme" was thus transposed to a type of "self-consciousness", where the thinking subject takes himself as a subject of reflection, where he thinks himself thinking himself, an endless process which of course is necessary self-transforming. From the standpoint of ontology, Leibniz proposed a doctrine of monads where each monad reflected the whole world from its own position, a world of which it is an integral part, implying that it reflects itself as well. In these different schemes, we are affected by a sense of infinite, which provokes a kind of vertigo, just like if we stood between a set of mirrors endlessly mirroring themselves. A dizziness that is amplified in the philosophical domain, since it is our very self which undergoes such a mysterious and paradoxical process of replication, distanciation and dissolution.

We clearly see in the present text how Zhuangzi induces self-consciousness through the "mise en abyme" of the subject that he is, speaking about himself both as a phenomenon, describing himself as a third person, and as well from the standpoint of a thinking subject, as an "I", or transcendental self, since he is the one speaking. But let us analyze this story and its relation to "mise en abyme" through the prism of the different characteristics defining such a process. Those characteristics all take on the paradoxical form of opposite concepts which create a tension within the process itself. For most of it, this paradoxical feature is grounded in the tension between the empirical self and the transcendent self, exposing the permanent tension these fundamental existential concepts undergo.

CLOSENESS AND DISTANTNESS The "mise en abyme" makes the subject simultaneously distant from himself, his empirical self, and closer to his transcendent self. By making himself the object of a dream, by speaking about himself in the third person, by becoming someone other than he is, in this case a butterfly, the author creates a distance from himself. But at the same time, he sees himself better, he understands himself better, since he becomes distant from himself. For example, he becomes conscious of the phenomenal nature of his person, he becomes aware of the superficial dimension of his immediate self, he realizes the transient feature of his existence, a wisdom which rings him closer to his true self.

VERTIGO AND STABILITY The "mise en abyme" launches a powerful process, shaking up the subject, putting him in an unsafe situation. At the same time, through this destabilization, he can reach "higher grounds", a form of stability gained from reaching this deeper or more elevated perspective. By envisaging the mere possibility of his life being actually a dream, through the new perspective of being someone else than he thought he was, thinking the unthinkable, one can indeed attain a more stable situation, where fixed conditions, obligations and identity are overcome, which implies that there is nothing anymore to fear, and nothing left to be desired, a condition for being with the Dao, according to Zhuangzi. But of course, in order to reach these "high grounds", one must go through a strong destabilization process, engendering dizziness and vertigo.

PRESENCE AND ABSENCE   The "mise en abyme" invites the subject
to play a game of hide and seek with himself. Most of the time, human beings are "inside" themselves, a "being in itself" as Sartre calls
it, in opposition of a "being for itself", rather conscious. They are so
close to themselves that they do not question so much this "self", they
take it as granted, as a must, as an inevitable condition for their own
existence. One could criticize this way of being as precisely a form of
alienation, alienation from "true self", from "conscious self", from "free
self". Sartre qualifies this state of mind or this being as having "bad
faith", since one gave up his fundamental freedom and consciousness
in order to play a role. A role that seems to impose itself on the individual, but which is in fact a choice, largely invested and overplayed as
a way to obtain a false sense of security. Zhuangzi invites us to break
away from those rituals we are plunged into, those rituals providing us
with status, well-being and social recognition, in order to rather enter
an appropriate ethical perspective. By abandoning ourselves, we can
become ourselves. Through breaking away from himself as Zhuangzi,
accepting that his life might be a dream, that he might be the production of a butterfly, Zhuangzi awakens to himself, the great awakening
that renders him present to himself.

ONE AND MULTIPLE   The "mise en abyme" engenders a situation,
or results from a situation, where the self is multiplied, either by producing new selves, through some kind of differentiated replication, or
by producing various images of the self. The problem here is that it
is difficult to distinguish between the self and its images, since one
could claim that the self is nothing but image. In a way, there is a
form of unity, since there is one consciousness, one identified subject,

and we have to presuppose some type of unity to speak about anything. At the same time, those different projections, those different components of the self, as Freud and others have identified it, make us doubt of this unity, either because the nature of it is hard to identify, or even because, forced by the strong evidence of the multiplicity, we have abandon even the mere possibility of such a reality as the "unity". Zhuangzi sleeps and dreams, Zhuangzi wakes up, Zhuangzi is a human, Zhuangzi is a butterfly. The unity of Zhuangzi is simultaneously presupposed and doubtful.

INSIDE AND OUTSIDE The "mise en abyme", through the interplay of the subject's multiple views, provokes an "alienation of the self": one is "expelled" from himself, while of course remaining himself. The relationship to one's image is precisely a relation of both "inside" and "outside". I am myself, but I see my image from outside. Paul Ricœur developed the idea of the double identity, by using two Latin words. "Ipse", is taking the self from the inside: it is the "I" which is at the center, the subject which transcends. "Idem", the identical, the similar: it is the "me", the "I" that makes itself an object; it is a projection, a construction. Kant opposes in the same way "thing in itself", the inner identity, and the "thing for itself", as a phenomenon, as it appears to the world. In the present story, Zhuangzi thinks, Zhuangzi writes, Zhuangzi dreams, he is inside himself, but he thinks, writes and dreams himself, he becomes an object for himself through the interplay of different images of himself.

RECOGNITION AND NON-RECOGNITION The "mise en abyme" provokes an estrangement of the self, where one at the same time recognizes himself, since many characteristics are identical in the self and the images, while recognizing that this "multiplicity of images" cannot be his self which is "one". He observes differences between those images and his self, already by the fact they are mere images or projections. Zhuangzi here insists on this contradictory dimension. The butterfly "knew nothing of Zhou", but then "at once he was Zhou", adding that "surely there is a difference between Zhou and a butterfly", but explaining this through "transformation of things", implying that they are therefore the same in some fashion. Although, strangely enough, through the "non-recognition", through the estrangement, one comes to recognize oneself better, what Zhuangzi calls the "great awakening". Through being other than yourself, you become yourself: that is the very idea of "mise en abyme".

ATTRACTION AND REPULSION   The "mise en abyme" produces both a cognitive and emotional effect upon the subject and the observer, a combination of pleasure and discomfort. The attraction is for one the fascination provoked by the kaleidoscopic effect of the multiplicity, purely esthetic. Second, the transformation, the playing with the self as an object, through its numerous projections, the differences it can engender, has an entertaining effect as well. The repulsion is on the other side provoked by a sensorial vertigo, since we are projected in the infinite. The experience of groundlessness can engender a sort of malaise, suspended that we are in some spatial or cognitive limbo, where nothing is established, nothing is sure, reality seems to vanish. Of course, this "vanishing" principle can captivate or enchant us, just like the experience of bungee jumping, to the extent we are confident, that we do not fear the loss of our self and our certitudes. That seems to be the case with Zhuangzi, who seems to gaily play with this "mise en abyme", which is part of his peaceful "roaming and soaring", where everything can be joyfully contemplated without any fear nor expectations.

Transformation of things

The conception of the cosmos common to all Chinese philosophy is neither materialistic nor animistic, since there are no soul substances. It can rather be called naturalistic, organic, or processual, even if some prefer to view it as magical or alchemical. The universe is viewed as a hierarchically organized organism in which every part reproduces the whole. The human being is a microcosm corresponding rigorously to this macrocosm, and even our body reproduces the plan of the cosmos. Therefore, between humans and the world exists a system of correspondences and participations that have been described at length in the tradition, for example in Chinese medicine. The basic genesis of the universe is that out the primordial chaos (Hundun) emerged the Dao, a law or principle, the natural order of things, which actually refers to the continuous engendering and reversion of everything to its starting point. A sort or breathing, in and out, or as a tide, rising and ebbing: all parts of the cosmos are attuned in a rhythmical pulsation. Nothing is static; all things are subjected to periodical mutations and transformations that represent the genesic process. Instead of being opposed to a static ideal, as we often encounter in western culture, change itself is the substance of reality: it is systematized and made intelligible, as in the 64 hexagrams of the Book of Changes (Yijing), which presents the main characteristics and conditions of the general flux. An unchanging unity, the constant Dao, underlies this kaleidoscopic plurality. The dynamic is one where everything accomplishes itself, goes to its own extreme, and then will invariably revert to its own contrary, to opposite qualities. "Reversion is the movement of the Dao", wrote Laozi. It reminds us as well of the neo-platonic principle of emanation and conversion: plurality comes from the primordial unity and returns to the primordial unity. Everything issues from the

Dao and ineluctably returns to it; undifferentiated unity becomes multiplicity in this process. Life and death are contained in this continuing transformation from Nothing into Something and back to Nothing, but the underlying primordial undefinable unity remains in the background. This implies a modality in the existence of things where the boundary between different things is periodically broken, one thing eternally transforming itself into another.

Even though this worldview corresponds well to the tradition, the term "transformation of things" actually comes from Zhuangzi. As we see in the present story, he thought that the boundary and difference between oneself and others, between being in a dream and being awake, and between all things, can be overcome. Consequently, one may always achieve the transformation between one thing and another. However, if one holds on avidly to the difference between oneself and the others, as in fear or greed, one cannot achieve the transformation of things, as if caught in a dream. But as well, because the mind is tricky, if one is bent too much on the transformation of things, one may still remain in another dream, what might call a "falling in the trap of one's own web". The ideal is to remain in a state of availability, what Zhuangzi calls "leisurely roaming", maintain oneself in an absence of direction and purpose. In this sense, one will erase the difference and opposition between the self and the universe. In Zhuangzi's view, status and etiquette, norms conventionally applied in the human world, the very act of naming and our fixed relation to language, cause divisions and antagonisms, and hence creates artificial and painful constraints on people. Namingly, in ancient Chinese thought, implied an evaluation assigning an object its place in a hierarchical universe. But the Dao escapes these categories, it is imperceptible, indiscernible, and of it nothing can be predicated. It latently contains the forms, the entities, the forces, the reality of all particular phenomena. Laozi writes: "It was from the "Nameless" that heaven and earth sprang. The "Named" is the mother that rears the "Ten Thousand Things" (all things), each after its kind." The "Nameless" (wuming) and the "Named" (youming), "Nothing" (wu) and "Something" (you), are interdependent and "grow out of one another." "Nothing" does not mean "Nothingness" but rather indeterminacy, the absence of perceptible qualities; in Laozi's view it is superior to "Something". It is the "Void" (empty incipience) that harbors, in itself, all potentialities and without which even "Something" lacks its efficacy. One should therefore omit status and norms, and even forget one's own physical existence and intellect, in order to cast off the differences between one's self and all else, and thus be free from the effect of external factors obscuring his thinking and affecting wrongly his behavior.

In On Seeing Things as Equal, Zhuangzi analyzes the unpredictable nature of the world to reveal that different or opposing things are inherently interconnected or even interchangeable. In striving to understand the world, one should therefore first of all identify the interconnectedness among all entities, seeing all as equal, and abandon personal preferences, likes and dislikes. In this way, one's heart can be above all material things, be liberated from outside constraints and influences; then the differences and contradictions among things will no longer burden one's mind or one's life. We ordinarily confine ourselves within our social roles, expectations, and values, with our everyday understandings of things. According to Zhuangzi, this way of acting is inadequate for a deeper appreciation of the nature of things, and for a more successful mode of interacting with them. We need to unlearn preconceptions that prevent us from seeing things and events in new ways; we need to see how we can structure and restructure the boundaries of things.

This unlearning can be viewed as an echo to the Socratic "learned ignorance", as Cusanus called it. But we can only do so when we ourselves have "wandered beyond" the boundaries of the familiar. It is only by freeing our imagination, in order to reconceive ourselves and our worlds, and the things with which we interact, that we may begin to understand the deeper tendencies of the natural transformations by which we are all affected, and of which we are all constituted. By loosening the bonds of our fixed presuppositions, we bring ourselves closer to an attunement to the potent and productive natural way of things. In order to resolve apparent contradictions, we must recognize the importance of continuous transformation underlying and uniting contrasting phenomena, we must perceive the unity between opposites. This implies to do away with the distinction between the self and the world, and to realize that life and death are but one of the pairs of cyclical phases, such as day and night or summer and winter. "Since life and death are each other's companions, why worry about them? All things are one." Life and death are not in opposition but merely two aspects of the same reality, arrested moments out of the flux of the ongoing mutations of everything into everything. Human beings are no exception: "They go back into the great weaving machine: thus all things issue from the loom and return to the loom." Zhuangzi's attitude thus is one of serene acceptance. In the tradition of Laozi's cosmology, Zhuangzi's worldview is one of seasonal transformations of opposites. The world is seen as a giant cloud (da kuai) around which the heavens (tian) revolve about a polar axis (daoshu). All transformations have such an axis, and the aim of the sage is to settle into this axis, so that one may observe the changes without being buffeted around by them. The concept Zhuangzi uses to capture this reality is the "pivot", the immobile part of the wheel that the whole wheel rotates around. This concept of "pivot" reminds us in a way of the Aristotelian concept of the unmoved mover, or prime mover, "that which moves without being moved", which he takes up as the primary cause of all things, the uncaused cause, the "mover" of all the motion in the universe, since it moves other things, but is not itself moved by any prior action. In addition to being motionless, the "first motor" is eternal, for if its existence had a beginning, it would need a cause. This monotheistic concept, coined by a polytheist, accounts for all transformations in the world, but it is as well described as the "thought of thought", as a Being which "thinks its own thinking". In that sense it is a pure form, an action without matter, which accounts for everything that is. The main difference between both philosophers seems to rely on the opposition between the concept of "cause" (Aristotle) and the one of "condition" (Zhuangzi). A cause fully accounts for the effects it produces, when a condition is a necessary structure, form or agent, although by itself it cannot totally account for the effects it produces. This difference is crucial in the distinction between "processual" Chinese thinking, and "creative" or "causal" Western thinking, although the distinction is far from being categorical. As well, another common point, Aristotle reminds us is that a "pair of opposites are born together". Although the principle of permanent interplay between differences and unity is more encountered in Heraclitus, his universal dynamic is rather more tense, agonistic and tragic than the one of Daoism, rather accepting and peaceful.

Evocation

In the Western thought there are established main different forms of speech: descriptive, prescriptive and performative. Descriptive is the speech that conveys a message about the "state" of the world to an interlocutor, it is a description of a thing, a phenomenon or an event, as we see from the name. Prescriptive speech gives a command, it conveys an order; through prescriptive speech one expresses what one thinks should be done, like in a medical prescription. Finally, performative speech is the one that makes a subject react and accomplish something in a rather indeterminate fashion, it prompts one to act upon the reality and modify it, without specifying this transformation. Performative discourse is not concerned with truth or falsehood of a given utterance, nor its utility: it is interested in the effect it produces. One can, of course, say that almost any speech is performative, as it forces an interlocutor to some kind of decision: to respond, to stay silent, to smile, to deny, etc. Even a word written on a shopping list can be considered performative, as it moves a subject to accomplish a certain action in relation to this word. Nevertheless, performative speech has significant features that distinguish it from other types of discourse. In a more striking way, it provokes a subject to start autonomous reflection: it does not convey a specific message or instruction, but stimulates a subject to respond or even transform oneself. Two recurrently met examples of performative speech in philosophical discourse are irony and paradox. Irony states the opposite of what is actually meant, or pretends a false reality like "ignorance", and by doing that, it makes a subject deal with the "double meaning" of a statement; it engenders ambiguity and groundlessness, where one will have to navigate without grasping any definitive signs or meaning of the original speech. Paradox, by combining contradictory ideas, creates the same destabilizing effect: it cannot offer a final conclusion as there is none. This is what Kierkegaard called "indirect communication": since existential or ontological truth cannot be simply described, it is not contained or transmitted by formal knowledge, it can only be "pounded out" of a subject. The process then follows an opposite direction to the one that descriptive speech accomplishes: one does not introduce, but one extracts; it is not "getting in", but "getting out".

Truth exists in a subject as a potential, as a capacity: it has to emerge. One therefore does not need to "plant" anything in the head of an interlocutor, one only needs to draw out what inevitably resides there. No wonder that Kierkegaard uses quite a strong verb to describe the process of extraction: "to pound out", which means that this truth is not a given and will appear only as a result of some clash; irony and paradoxical message fitting this purpose well. Usage of performative discourse indicates that the one who creates an effect trusts that he will find an echo in his interlocutor, by communicating what is implied and invisible. Indirect communication forces the interlocutor to take a decision by himself through combining contradictory information. In such an act the one emitting performative discourse will temporarily cease to exist, as he will not occupy any fixed position or will not have some specific content to defend: himself and what he says can be viewed through multiple perspectives, depending on how one wants to regard it. Through momentary reduction of oneself to "no one", a bearer of performative speech gives liberty to his protagonist to do as he wishes, inciting autonomous action, and as a consequence existential freedom. Unlike in the case of direct demand for taking a position on a specific issue, the launching of a formulation with double or multiple meaning will in a more evident way place the opposing subject at a crossroads, where he will not be able to determine clearly which way is the "correct" one, just like he will not be able to guess what his interlocutor thinks. Socratic irony, for example, had this effect: there was at the same time a direct question requiring an answer, and a "second layer" of ironic attitude, where Socrates would present himself as ignorant or praise suspiciously his interlocutor. These moves could have been both "true" and "false", taken as face value or not, and it is what forced his interlocutors, taken aback, to define their own stance. This could partially explain as well the reactions of indignation and irritation of the "opponent", caught between a feeling of indetermination and the demand for the production of a clear-cut judgement.

In the Eastern thought, more specifically in the words of Zhuangzi, there is in addition another type of speech, called "evocative speech", that lets things be accomplished through an "invitation", but not through a direct request. Irony, in this system of thought, belongs to the category of evocative and not performative speech, although the distinction between the two seems to be rather vague. An important example of evocative discourse that can more separate itself from other forms of communication is the metaphorical mode of expression that is quite recurrent in the Chinese way of thinking. Things are said indirectly, without being really said, everything is a mere hint that can be interpreted differently. Even the structure of Chinese language is evocative: one ideogram can carry dozens of meanings, some contradicting one another. The language has no tenses or genders, and in the case of old Chinese idiom even no prepositions, all this leading to a large variety of interpretations and assigned meanings. What has only one straightforward meaning even loses any interest, as it does not open a field of possible interpretations: it can be considered banal and mundane, almost primitive, as it designates exactly what it intends to designate. So even everyday language should preferably be indirect and by being so, engender production of multiple meanings.

Zhuangzi proposes three modalities of discourse: 寓言 (yuyan), which means "dwelling words" or "imputed words" that he claims to take nine-tenths of the text, 重言 (zhongyuan), the "repeated words" or "expert words", that make seven-tenths of the text, and then the third type, 卮言–"goblet words" that he claims: "come forth day after day, harmonizing things in the Heavenly Equality". The first type represents what people tell themselves on an everyday basis, when they simply want to express what preoccupies them and want to be understood. Zhuangzi writes that they "respond only to what agrees with their own views and reject what does not": what is right and what is wrong then correspond to their opinions. They have no distance with themselves and do not wish to search for truth outside of their perspective. This seems to be the most widespread relation to words. The second type are the words that "put an end to an argument" because they are "referenced": they are pronounced by the elderly or by an authority. Zhuangzi here criticizes formal reverence just as the first category does, since it is not so preoccupied with the way things are, but only to "prove a point" and to convince others. He criticizes the reference to "antiquity" and advises to look at "old texts" as "a mere stale remnant of the past". Unless there is something establishing that the content or the author is somehow "ahead of others" in its way of being. The third type of words are the most interesting one, and of course the rarest one: "goblet words". These words function like a goblet: it tips itself when full and rights itself when empty. We should specify that the name "goblet" refers to a specific type of metal cup the ancient Chinese used, where the bottom is not flat but somewhat rounded, which therefore should not be filled too much otherwise it tilts and spills over. Therefore, the liquid comes naturally in and out of this unstable object. Then the specificity of these "goblet words" is that they "go along" with nature, fitting what the author calls "harmonizing all things", a form of adaptation or availability.

We notice that the content of what Zhuangzi writes, the form and style he uses, corresponds to the meaning of the message he conveys, that is the absence of any particular message. His semantics are quite troubling. In his speech, a signifier is often distant from the signified, one word is used to express another word. His discourse is saturated with figurative descriptions and multiple dialogues, so there is no direct message, but meaning hides itself in various metaphors. One metaphor points to the other one and so on endlessly. It never arrives at a final specific idea, always being circular: once one meaning is attained, there is another one luring at the horizon; a mise en abyme that knows no end. For example, Zhuangzi introduces all kinds of different creatures that interact with each other, leaving the interpretation of their dialogues to the reader: cicadas, snakes, butterfly, shadow, etc. There is a cascade of meanings that one can extract from these dialogues; the reader is supposed to move amidst different metaphors that will present themselves endlessly. Even when important people are speaking in dialogues, their authority is doubtful: what is said should not be taken literally: "experts" do not propose any clear-cut positions, they offer paradoxes, sometimes the presentation is ironical, so the reader is forced to go through the meanderings of thought in order to make up his own mind, which is mind boggling for interpreters of Zhuangzi. At no point does the metaphorizing stop. There is an effect of dissipation of authoritative weight on the mind of a reader, as instead of reading the "true word", one sees how meanings and ideas intertwine and form paradoxes. There are no traces of the absolute truth, but playfulness and freedom. In this sense there is de-subjectivization of words, since no one in particular is responsible for them, and the reader is free – and forced to initiate an autonomous reflection. There is as well a de-substantialization, since the "official" signification is taken away from the signifier. There is a call for self-involvement, which means that an interlocutor will be thrown back to himself, his understanding will be convoked and brought in by him, not by an outside authority. Because of this, there is a recurrent misinterpretation of Zhuangzi texts: some take too seriously what he says, others take it too lightly, some complicate the texts to the extent they become unrecognizable, some "mystify" him in a religious way. This phenomenon is an obvious consequence of the potential multiplicity of interpretations that any text of his conveys. Once a reader is given the freedom to decipher an idea the way he wants, he can easily abuse this freedom, or on the reverse neglect it.

The butterfly story is an excellent representation in action of the "goblet words" that Zhuangzi speaks about: "Once Zhuang Zhou dreamt he was a butterfly, a butterfly fluttering gaily. He enjoyed himself very much and he knew nothing of Zhou. Suddenly, he awoke, and all at once he was Zhou. But he did not know whether Zhou had dreamt about being a butterfly or a butterfly had dreamt about being Zhou. Surely there is a difference between Zhou and a butterfly. This is what we call the transformation of things!" An innocent and very short story, no explanation followed, no indication of what to make out of it. The common version most recurrently told omits the idea of transformation of things, leaving only the funny wondering of Zhuangzi about his identity. But the transformation is at the heart of the story. The content of the story coincides with the way Zhuangzi relates to the language: goblet writings leave things "to their endless changes", not fixating on anything, only issuing an invitation to a reader to self-involve and joyfully roam together with the text, not seeking any definite point, not having final destination. Such discourse wants the reader to be initiated to a new meaning, but not impose it, since such imposition is impossible anyhow. The principle of such a pedagogy is that what is proposed by an outside figure will forever remain on the outside, unless lived and experienced. This is probably why Zhuangzi prefers to tell stories instead of making explanatory speeches. Story is a miniature of life, a place with multi-directions where a reader can wonder and choose his path: he is free to explore. But the poor reader faces an "excess" of figurative meanings, and metaphors, which can be quite discouraging at first glance, as we personally experienced. And the fact there is no "break" from one metaphor to the text, one short text flowing into a distinct one, one transformation following another one, can infuriate some who search for one definite meaning, accusing Zhuangzi of too much frivolity and absence of substance. There is no fixed identity of the author in the story of the butterfly, just like there is no fixed meaning in the story. Zhuangzi is first himself dreaming of being a butterfly and then a butterfly dreaming of being Zhuangzi: it is not clear who is the "real" self, as there is no "real" self, only interdependence of things, and no fixed ground.

Such a way of communication seeks to bring a new realization that is not an accumulation of knowledge, but a transformation in one's being. The more one can wonder among multiple perspectives, the more one can grow richer in one's perception of the world. Wondering will never stop, as it goes along with the nature of things. Goblet words are the reflection of Dao: ungraspable, never-ending, transforming, elusive. They never point directly at an object, but always send the reader someplace else. This way the subject –content and reader–has a chance to become "worldly", enlarging oneself, as one flutters like a butterfly from one metaphor to the next. Such an expansion cannot take place through gathering of data and reading about perspectives, it can only pass through an experience of "living it". Through such indirect communication a subject is plunged into a plurality of angles and this way "pounded out" of his natural unilateral standpoint. Once he is roaming in the multiplicity of perspectives, he will approach closer to the natural order of things and by doing so will help understanding and expressing reality. It is a mutual process, a reciprocal interdependence: a subject should open to the world in order to become worldly and the world then opens to a subject, emerging through it. It is impossible to know whether it is a reader that reads the world, or if it is the world that reads the reader. Language in this way is perceived as a stage where various sides of the world meet and interact with one another, and through this, the "piping of heaven" becomes visible, a spirit that blows throughout of the universe, that is distinguished from the "piping of earth", the music of nature, such as the wind blowing through the trees, and the "piping of humans", for example playing a flute.

It makes no sense to attempt to state what Zhuangzi "really" thinks, as for the reasons listed above it would go against the purpose of what he is saying. His speech introduces the reader to a permanent state of in-betweenness. Through the usage of irony, he pulls the carpet from under the reader's feet. Irony does not state anything without denying it the next moment. What is meant by a statement is in fact refuted by what this statement says. What is stated contradicts what is implied, what is implied contradicts what is stated and so on. The butterfly story is ironic in this sense: the identity of the butterfly denies the identity of Zhuangzi and the reverse, one can never know what is "more real" and a demand for such knowledge does not even make sense. One does not simply receive a message that a notion of identity can only be conceived through a notion of transformation, but one is put in a position where one starts to perceive it and relive it.

A metaphor "walks two", as it pronounces two things at the same time: "what is said" and "what is not said". In this sense any metaphor is ironic. There is a simultaneous denial of "what is said", since there is a reference to something else, and the words even come to bear a superfluous dimension as well. Zhuangzi wrote that "everything is a horse", in order to express the power of the metaphor, implying that anything can be transposed to anything else. The strictness of a definition would only prohibit actual understanding and would bring one farther away from the order of the universe. If something is only "what it is", it would prohibit one from seeing this thing, as it should be seen as a part of all things. One can criticize such an approach, saying that it leads to chaos and constant over interpretation, as one is left on its own, free to assign any meaning one wants. As would object scholars who claim they "need" precision of definition. Of course, if one does not have a habit of interpretation, one will simply project one's usual way of looking at things. This explains the multiplicity of interpretations of Zhuangzi. One can respond back by claiming that the existence of these interpretations is precisely what moves thinking, what makes the variety of perspectives possible, what brings a text to life.

If nature is fundamentally metaphorical, if nothing is what it is but something else as well, then the only way of expressing it would be through a metaphor. Nature is multi-faceted and dynamic: it is not rigid and fixed in one form of self-expression; matter, shapes and forms are being constantly transformed, everything is in the state of becoming, one seed contains a potential of a plant, one season contains a potential of another one. If a subject approaches such a process of transformation with one particular or definite vision, and through the language solidifies the becoming, one will remain in the illusion of understanding that will in no way approach the natural ordering of things. One therefore should apply an instrument that coincides in its structure with what it deals with. If one thinks through the concept of "goblet words", one can actually become the change itself and partake in the ontological transformation of things, being in-between Zhuangzi and the butterfly, becoming the "glass of all things".

Participation in the order of things that passes through "goblet words" is not merely a theoretical matter to entertain one's mind, it has direct consequences on the way one lives one's life. It is not a life regulated by "moral injunctions" with a checklist of what is allowed and what is not, it is not a life with a proclaimed ideal and the expectation of reaching this ideal, it is a life of roaming and soaring in the world, acting upon reality and listening to its responses, being a part of the transformation processes. It is therefore not an agonistic and agonizing struggle, but a pleasant and vigorous wondering. It is then a life not ruled by the external judging eye of another person, or the one of society, but the aspiration coming out of internal necessity, in other words, driven by inner joy.

Goblet words are not preoccupied with themselves, with their meaning and intention, all attention is directed outside, to an interlocutor. And even if such words are senseless or absurd, as long as they create an effect in others, strangely enough they will have meaning: this is their performative power. In this sense an ironist "does not exist", both from a standpoint of the negation of his own words, and from the standpoint of being directed at his interlocutor rather than at himself. Thus, he is neither attached to the content of what he is saying, nor to his status. He is a joker. He is nowhere, always on the move, on the brink, inviting his interlocutor to follow him in his endeavor. A good ironist should in a way be misunderstood, it is a mark of a good irony. It means that he managed to let another person cut loose, to incite in him the freedom to choose his own path. Although reaching this light attitude of fluttering in the world is not as easy as it might seem. In Zhuangzian ethics, one should be available to anything that comes in one's way, one should know how to let go of one's anxiety over the loss of one's own identity, one should let oneself get lost without any hope of finding oneself back, one should be able to stand the indetermination of transformation from being at the same time a butterfly and oneself.

The great awakening

Both dreams of the story are connected, Zhuangzi dreams and the butterfly dreams, even though they are of quite different nature, and are mutually exclusive. The way they are connected is from "outside", from the passage between them, from the global process which transcends them, what is called the "great awakening": the practice of emerging from different "little awakenings", which implies to realize the "dream" or "dreams" we are plunged into, each one with its "own integrity and reality". We are actually invited by Zhuangzi to "awaken on the awakening", since each awakening does not "settle the issue". Each dream should produce its own doubt and uncertainty, each dream is disqualified by its "outside", until the self itself becomes disqualified. The ideal observer should be totally severed from the world, a rather impossible endeavor, but a powerful regulatory ideal, since one cannot in the absolute extract himself from himself. As a stop-gap measure, one can use this back and forth shuttle between dreams, in order not to get stuck in a fixed scheme or paradigm. From this standpoint, the different dreams need each other, they are interdependent. Just like the confrontation of different positioning allows us to maintain a dialectical posture, a distance from ourselves, what is called the "mise en abyme", looking at ourselves in the perspective of infinity or nothingness.

Once we consider that everything is a dream, that "life is nothing but a dream within a dream", as Edgar Allan Poe phrases it, then we make ourselves "hollow", allowing for the "celestial piping", as Zhuangzi calls it. From this position, we can "think things without being thinged by things", because we are not a prisoner of ourselves and of our representations: we become free and powerful through our plasticity and emptiness. Moving between worlds engenders stability, contrary to what we normally and instinctively presupposed, a very counterintuitive attitude. From this transcendent standpoint, "all things are equal", not because their values are equal, but because they are all the mere mutually necessary means for a higher order reality. The relation between those opposed "dreams" is therefore peaceful and non-agonistic, a major difference between Zhuangzi and Western dialectics, where the confrontation between opposites, negativity, is endowed with passion, conflict and even suffering. The indecisive setting this places the reader into can be perceived as rather uneasy, but it can as well be enjoyed as a "leisurely meandering", as proposed by Zhuangzi, a good approximation of the "human Dao".

One should not make the mistake of viewing this description as a denial of reality, quite the contrary. In opposition to Buddhist philosophy, where all is "maya" (illusion) beside the vacuity, for Zhuangzi and most Daoist thinkers, this on the contrary constitutes reality. Flexibility is the condition for perception of reality, since plasticity is of the essence of the Dao, engendered by chaos. Of course, the grounding in the "non-ground" can give us the impression of a vanishing reality, but it allows us in fact to come closer to the "pivot", the center around which all rotate. This reminds us of Nicholas of Cusa, the 15th century philosopher, for whom all ideas are mere conjectures, through which we can slowly approximate the fundamental reality of things. For him the center is God, the "non-other", since it is not "other" than anything, in opposition to all things or beings which are what they are because precisely they are "other" than something else: they have an identity. This center is for him "the circle whose center is everywhere and its circumference is nowhere". This reminds us very much of the idea of the "pivot", which does not move but makes everything rotate.

The dream is not an illusion, it is simply a changing and ephemeral phenomenon that can only lead to another one, unless we become a prisoner of it. The world is an infinite roaming of subjects, like in the "monadology" of Leibniz, where each entity contains in its own modality the totality of the universe, a universe composed by an infinity of monads. An infinite process of mutual determinations. Natural order is a permanent alteration of "this and that", apparently fixed things which oppose each other and relate in an external fashion, although internally they are tightly interconnected. But within all this movement, which might appear chaotic, within this "back and forth" of numerous cycles, in this constant changeover among things, we can notice the "great transformation" (wu hua), we can hear the "heavenly piping", perceive the "pivot". In this puzzling game of hide and seek of the "same and different", we can intuit the Dao. At the same time, dream and reality cannot be the same, Zhuangzi is keen to not maintain some undifferentiated or relativistic world outlook, where thinking and reality would be de facto banned, as devoid of reality or substance. There is a coincidence of opposites in the absolute, in the "great awakening", in the "awakening of awakening", where the perspective is actually empty, but that is not to deny the "this and that", otherwise we would enter a world where "the night where all the cows are black", as Hegel calls it.

The choice of the butterfly as the animal "object" and "subject" of the dream is not an accident. The free fluttering of this lively, beautiful, and light insect symbolizes the permanent change of identities. Reasoning is not its cup of tea: this task is left to Zhuangzi and the reader. Thinking is precisely a "dream", and absence of reality, for the poor butterfly; its identity, its "De" is elsewhere, and that is why it is offering an interesting counterpoint to those "heavy thinking humans", who "cling" instead of "fluttering". The butterfly is never at rest in its flip-flopping, therefore shaking the foundation of judgment and self. It is a spontaneous creature, and paradoxically enough, "great awakening" and "spontaneity" have something in common: the impossibility of knowledge or consciousness. The first one because it is beyond any separation or judgment, since all is one. The second one because it "does not care" about judgment, since judgment is discursive, argumentative, when the butterfly, at least as we perceive it, is in the immediate.

In Western philosophy and in common thinking, there is the quest for a mysterious and unchanging subject, an identity, the singular foundation for our existence. It can be called an "ego-logical" type of thinking. For example the indubitable ego of Descartes, the entity that "thinks" or "doubts", or Kant's transcendental ego, the subject that unites all perception and thoughts, the condition of possibility of any cognitive activity. Many philosophers have attempted to define such an unquestionable foundation for the self. Although others, especially in the recent period, have instilled doubt in such a unity, like Hume or Freud. But Zhuangzi is rather concerned with dissolving the subject as a condition for an adequate epistemological and ontological perspective, more fitting his Daoist perspective. But we must here warn the reader about a tempting mistake: the idea is not to totally abolish the subject, to radically deny the "this and that", but simply to abolish the fixed standpoint, to multiply the standpoints in order to avoid any dogmatism and rigidity. To be "selfless" is not to abandon the world.On the other side, it is to be more open to the world, to be more available, more present to reality, to be able to welcome the multiplicity of things. Like the condition for a true self. The "great awakening" is not the abandon of any "thought", but it is modifying the way we relate to our "thoughts". We cannot abandon our "dreams", but we have to remain conscious that "dreams are dreams", and we have to keep dreaming, otherwise we are threatened with falling into dogmatism. In a way, we have to maintain both a "critical" and an "a-critical" attitude. A-critical in the sense of being available to multiplicity, welcoming the diversity, no matter how strange or surprising it is. "Critical" in the sense of evaluating, judging, and comparing each "dream", for its worth and for its limits. We should not give up on distinguishing phenomena, we should acquiesce and confirm "what is" and "what happens", but contemplate and analyze it in the perspective of the "Dao" or the "Great awakening", where life and death are two facets of the same coin, like consciousness and unconsciousness.

There is darkness in Zhuangzi, but his darkness is not despair, as for example in the tragic or absurd writings of Albert Camus or Kierkegaard, but simply the nocturnal background of a nonchalant roaming. It is not the somber mystery of the soul, but the short night that precedes and succeeds the day. In its long years of roaming, Odysseus sadly dreamed of coming back to Ithaca, Sisyphus desperately hoped to see the rock finally reaching the heavens. The world of Zhuangzi is not unidirectional, it does not long for some earthly or celestial paradise. He promotes a vision of multiple horizons, animated by a dynamic process, with ceaseless and constant reversal of dependence. There is no fixed ground in his ontological dynamism. For this reason, we have to learn "selfless unknowing", an example given by the butterfly, who has neither identity, nor grounding, nor knowledge. In his permanent fluttering, he is a non-subject, and a brainless creature. The whole story is a dream, and it leaves the reader perplexed. Those who do not know what to do with this story, besides finding it "cute", "funny" or "strange". But for once he can understand and remember a Zhuangzian incongruity, which will then explain why the present text is the only one from our author that has gained some popularity throughout the ages.

Comprehension questions

1. Why does Zhou no longer know if he is Zhou or the butterfly?

2. What is Zhou's relationship to the butterfly?

3. Is Zhou's dream a reality?

4. Who is Zhou?

5. What is the difference between Zhou and the butterfly?

6. What similarity is there between Zhou and the butterfly?

7. What does this dream teach us about the reality of things?

8. Why is the butterfly ignorant of Zhou?

9. What is the relationship in this story between dreams and ignorance?

10. What does Zhou's dream mean?

Reflection questions

1. Why are human beings looking for an identity?

2. Do animals have an identity?

3. Can we really know others?

4. Can you be someone other than yourself?

5. Is the dream a component of identity?

6. Should we trust our dreams?

7. Is a dream a form of thought?

8. Do dreams help us to know ourselves?

9. Is our existence a dream?

10. Do we prefer to be ourselves or someone else?

Mastering life

Tien Kai-chih went to see Duke Wei of Chou. Duke Wei said, "I hear that Chu Hsien is studying how to live. You are a friend of his –what have you heard from him on the subject?" Tien Kai-chih said, "I merely wield a broom and tend his gate and garden –how should I have heard anything from the Master?" Duke Wei said, "Do not be modest, Master Tien. I am anxious to hear about it." Tien Kai-chih said, "I have heard the Master say, 'He who is good at nourishing life is like a herder of sheep –he watches for stragglers and whips them up.'" "What does that mean?" asked Duke Wei. Tien Kai-chih said, "In Lu there was Shan Pao –he lived among the cliffs, drank only water, and did not go after gain like other people. He went along like that for seventy years and still had the complexion of a little child. Unfortunately, he met a hungry tiger who killed him and ate him up. Then there was Chang Yi –there was not one of the great families and fancy mansions that he did not rush off to visit. He went along like that for forty years, and then he developed an internal fever, fell ill, and died. Shan Pao looked after what was on the inside and the tiger ate up his outside. Chang Yi looked after what was on the outside and the sickness attacked him from the inside. Both these men failed to give a lash to the stragglers." Confucius has said, "Do not go in and hide; do not come out and shine;

stand stock-still in the middle. He who can follow these three rules is sure to be called the finest."

Empirical self

Zhuangzi opposes two aspects of the person, as an individual: the "inside", what Shan Pao cared about and favored, and the "outside", what Chang Yi looked after and favored. In the western philosophical tradition, one way to distinguish those two dimensions of the self is called the opposition between the "transcendental subject" and the "empirical subject".

But let us first briefly examine the concept of subject.

The subject is first of all a concept of logic or language: it is the part of the proposition to which a predicate is attributed. For example, in "the ball is round", ball is the subject, round is the predicate, the way the ball "is". In metaphysics, the subject is the "being" or "substance", some fundamental and rather invariant entity, to which we attribute qualities, conceived as the cause of specific actions. Therefore, the subject is for one an object of thought and knowledge, a judgment, since it has as a primary function to construct our understanding and mastery of the world. Second, the subject is the ontological support of numerous realities, such as action, consciousness, perception, relation or else, the substrate on which those features are anchored. From both these standpoints, we observe the crucial function of such a concept in both language and thought, in order to grasp reality and describe it. When we come to the "human subject", the issue becomes more specific and complex, since we deal with "a subject that thinks itself". This situation provokes a sort of conundrum, since we are both judge and party in the matter, as we think this subject from the "inside", as "I", or "we", and from the outside, as "me", "you" or "them". The first one is the cause of the thinking, it freely produces it, it is the reflexive subject, or transcendental self, when the second one is the product or object of the thinking, the consequence of this thinking, the empirical self.

Let us in this first part examine what constitutes the empirical self, the outside with what Chang Yi is concerned. The empirical basically designates what can be noticed by any external observer, what is inscribed in space and time, since it has direct physical manifestations, producing identifiable signs. Zhuangzi writes about Chang Yi: "there was not one of the great families and fancy mansions that he did not rush off to visit". What do we therefore know about this man? We can identify some obvious characteristics through this short description, as probable presuppositions of his psychological nature and activity: he is a greedy, ambitious, relational, utilitarian, impatient and rather corrupted person. Through his actions, we forcibly notice someone oriented towards status and the possession of material wealth. Sartre would tell us that this is the essential of his being, since according to the text this is the concrete purpose to which he dedicates his life. He is therefore an outer oriented person, with no fundamental preoccupation for the "intrinsic quality" of his own self. Zhuangzi names this characteristic "intention", what we would now call subjectivity. A subjectivity connected to "having" rather than "being". To have or to be? is the title of a book by Erich Fromm, which captures the essence of a classical ethical dilemma. For this author, the choice that humanity will make between these two modes of existence determines its very nature and survival. Because our world is more and more dominated by the passion of having, focused on acquisitiveness, the desire of possession, material power, aggressiveness, in opposition to the mode of the being, founded on love, spiritual fulfillment, the pleasure of sharing meaningful and fruitful activities. He concludes that if man does

not realize the seriousness of this choice, he will run to an unprece-
dented psychological and ecological disaster.

The empirical nature of the subject can be known by others, and
even through others: we could literally observe in the behavior of
Chang Yi what Zhuangzi describes: we could film it with a camera.
The empirical self can take the form of a narration, the recounting of
a series of actions and events. In opposition to mysterious internal
processes, we can know with a relative certitude the reality of the person. We can ignore the intricacies of his mental processes, we can be
mistaken on his particular intentions at a given moment, but through
certain behavioral patterns, to a large extent we still have access to
the concrete nature of his self. We can of course perceive a person's
material self. For one, his biological characteristics, such as gender,
age, height, weight, agility. Second, his actions and the result of his
actions, such as what he owns, his function and status, his education,
his social interactions. Third, his environment, such as his family, his
friends, his social context. Fourth, his intellectual and emotional life,
such as his interests, his passions, his desires and fears. As observers,
we can more or less identify those characteristics, and to the extent
the subject is willing to do so, he can do it as well.

But we encounter some problems when we know a subject through
the empirical nature of his self. First of all, a number of those characteristics necessarily change, willy-nilly, such as age or appearance,
some most likely change, like interests or activities, and others might
change, depending on the context or internal changes of the subject,
like pursuits or emotions. As a consequence of those changes, the
knowledge becomes doubtful in relation to "knowing the person", since
identifying any entity presupposes some rather unchanging characteristics. And of course, any particular individual is engaged in numer-

ous activities that can be quite different or even radically opposed, either within the same time frame, or at least over an extended period. We often observe how time can dramatically affect someone's behavior, with the consequence of doubting about the "fundamental reality" of this person. The second problem is the interaction between the context and the subject, what can be called the heteronomy of the empirical subject, a non-autonomous self, since his "reality" is largely determined by the outside. This phenomenon takes place in two ways, one which can be called passive, the other one active. The passive way refers to the modifications we undergo when the context changes, affecting the way of being of the subject. The active way refers to the way the subject will modify his behavior to protect himself or to obtain what he wants: for example, he will be harsh with hierarchical inferiors but pleasing with superiors, in order to satisfy their wishes, or he will be tough in business relations and tender in family matters, since both types of bonding have for him different functions. As well, a teacher will adapt his pedagogy depending on the type of students he has, the flexibility of differentiated pedagogy being the characteristic of a good teacher. One can of course find some unity or coherence in those different cases, but from a purely empirical standpoint, one can observe objective differences or oppositions. Therefore, the empirical subject is changeable since he is multiple. His behavior is determined by the perception he has of the world at a given moment. And in the same way he is affected by the sensation of his own internal states at any given moment, what can be called his "moods", shifting for physiological or psychological reasons. From this, although the empirical reality of the subject is quite concrete, his "identity" becomes difficult to define.

One other helpful insight about the empirical self is brought about by the "ego" concept of Freud. The founder of psychoanalysis, the "talking cure", established a tripartition of the self: id (this), ego (me), and super-ego (super-me). They represent three distinct yet interacting agents constituting the psychic apparatus. According to this model, the id is the set of uncoordinated instinctual trends, rejections and desires, the super-ego plays the critical, idealistic and moralizing role, while the ego is the organized, pragmatic part that mediates between the drives of both the id and the super-ego, a sort of intermediary that interacts with the reality of the world. The ego is the emerging part of the self, empirical, facing the outside, undergoing pressure from two conflicting centers of pressure. On one side a sort of "pit" of archaic, biological and more superficial cravings determining what we "desire", on the other side a set of personal and socially constructed regulatory ideals establishing what we "should be" or "should want". The empirical self is pleased to satisfy his irrational desires, but he has to resist their satisfaction because their unbridled demands go against social norms and against ideal norms, both of which have to be satisfied as well, for practical and psychological reasons.

Thus, Chang Yi was visibly driven by greed and ambition, his empirical self was concentrated on getting wealth, fame and power, since he put a lot of effort all his life to interact with wealthy, famous and powerful persons. But he could not just take directly from others what he wanted in order to satisfy those needs and impulses: he had to satisfy social rules and conditions, please his environment in order to get what he wanted, either to seduce them, to manipulate them or to confront them in an adequate manner. Whence the importance of the heteronomy, the outward determination, which necessarily indicates a certain existential or moral "corruption", since the subject modifies, curbs and suppresses his "natural being" in order to fit the "outside". Moreover, he pays the price for this corruption: the permanent display of his self upon the world is accompanied with a constant worry of failing his show, with the threat of not gaining what he wants, with the fear of losing what he already has. He as well transformed those impulses, he constrained and channeled them in order to satisfy whatever "ideal", moral, existential, esthetic or intellectual, he and his environment had built up for himself. For example, having a "good" family, helping "generously" some persons, having a "beautiful" house, behaving in a formally "respectful" manner, in other words trying to satisfy some values that would make his self "worthy" in his own eyes. Thus, the production of his own being would be, or rather try to be a "balance" between those diverse conflicting forces. A "balance" that most likely would be illusory, since those opposite "forces" bear too much opposition between themselves. From there, human existence is often one of doubt, anxiety and deception.

Transcendent self

If the empirical self is outer-oriented and heteronomous, the transcendent self is rather inner-oriented and autonomous. Although the distinction between these "selves", in terms of nature, motivation, action or dynamic is not always so clear: they can periodically conflate or overlap. But let us anyhow try to examine further how to distinguish them, by now analyzing how to characterize the transcendent subject. One classical way to identify this entity is through consciousness, otherwise defined as the capacity to unify representations: feelings, knowledge, judgments, etc. Our mind would be scattered, there would be no coherency, if we were not capable to relate all those activities and data to one common center: the "I", which is the entity or "center" undergoing those process or provoking those processes.

Consciousness refers to the state of being awake and aware of one's surroundings, which implies that there is "something", some "autonomous entity", which is awake and aware. Thus, it is concluded that in general this "perception" can and should be attributed to a subject, since it is difficult to conceive of a subject-less consciousness. Even if we think of the whole universe as conscious of itself, such a phenomenon will necessarily take place through certain entities more than others, since this universe is differentiated. Then we attribute the faculty of awareness to something called the mind, for there must be in a complex being some center which specializes more in this activity, as for any other activity. Finally, we arrive at the idea of an organ, mind, brain, soul or else, which is conscious of both itself and the world. Further on, if this is the case, this mind, or the being endowed with this mind, has to be able to think or say "I", for two reasons. First, as we saw, it is a singular being: something distinguishes this entity from the other entities through a very specialized and important function. Second, it is not some object we think about from the outside, as distant, but a "oneself", the fact something is both cause and consequence, active and passive, the reflective and reflexive function "covered" by the term "I". One should notice how a child takes some years before he can use the term "I": at first, he speaks about himself as someone else, "John wants···", from the standpoint of parents or other adults, as an "object", until he discovers the paradoxical and autonomous function of the "I". "Before saying 'I' the child had only the feeling of himself, now he has the thought of it", wrote Kant. Using this simple pronoun concretizes the subject's ability to represent himself as a single entity: to be a subject is to have the capacity of unifying numerous representations, active and passive, what can be called "the unifying power of consciousness", a human privilege. This activity, power, or spiritual organ, can be called the transcendent self, an elusive but necessary condition of our human existence.

There are different ways to conceive the "subject", which we will for now take as a synonym of "transcendent self". It can be understood by different modalities. It can be conceived as a simple cause of action, like in "the stone made the noise when it fell", where the stone just underwent passively the law of gravitation, but still was a cause producing an effect. Then it can be conceived as a "willful" cause, like in "The bird ate the seed", where the bird acted singularly on the basis of his instinct. Finally, it can be viewed as a "deliberate" cause, like in "Peter decided to become a carpenter". The degree of freedom is maximized in the last case, in a gradation where the "subject" becomes more and more of a "subject": it is "subjectivized" through his increasing degrees of autonomy. From this, we could even go further in the process by stating, as Spinoza, Kant and others, that freedom is acquired further through an increase in the degree of consciousness. For this, we would have to examine how much Peter knows about carpentry, and what are his motivations for becoming a carpenter, in order to determine the nature, validity and autonomy of his "decision", establishing his degree of freedom and therefore his status as a subject. From this, we can affirm that a "true" subject has consciousness of himself, he is self-conscious, since he is part of reality and knows himself. From this we define a subject which is actually free since he even defines himself, he makes himself be what he decides to be. This freedom of self-determination is used of course as a comparative statement, not as an absolute, since one will object here that our power in this domain is not without strong restrictions.

Thus the « I » symbolizes or expresses the fact man possesses the capacity to direct himself, by designating himself as being endowed with reason. Reason refers to the reflexive capacity of analyzing a situation, taking a decision and undertaking an action. Descartes is famous as one of the first philosophers, if not the first, to identify this "I", in his "Cogito" principle. It can be basically summarized in the idea that one can doubt everything, including the existence of God and the universe, but one cannot doubt the fact he doubts. Thus, if everything can be illusory, the "thinking I" escapes such a fate, and the transcendent self becomes the only evidence we can "cling" to. Kant entertains a different perspective, rather the opposite, that the transcendent self is not knowable, since it cannot be the object of any true experience. For him, only the phenomenon can be actually known, information which can be obtained through sense perception. In opposition, the noumena, a pure abstraction, can only be the object of an "intellectual intuition". It is for him associated with something "negative", since the human is actually limited to knowledge defined by space and time, meaning to "sensitive intuition". He of course admits that the "transcendent self" thinks, but he claims that it does not know what it is: it cannot define itself; it can only logically presuppose its own presence through the unifying action of thought. He rejects the idea of Plato and other idealist philosophers according to which we can have a direct and intuitive access to the "world of ideas", to the "intelligible world". What objects are in themselves is out of reach for us, we only know their manifestation: the phenomenon, from which he concludes we can only know the empirical self. Although he recognizes the difficulty this represents for us, since the empirical self is changing, it is multiple, it is affected by the sensations of his own internal states, which makes it difficult to discern as well. Each self has its own different motives and goals, which could even be a source of internal conflict. We can analyze in someone his psychology, his behavior, but not the nature of what is united, free and intemporal, the transcendental self, often called the soul.

In opposition to this, there is a long tradition of idealist philosophers who think that this transcendental self is the fundamental anchorage that we can reach, care about and to which we must aspire, in order to realize oneself. An enlightening example is Augustine, who wrote that God is our most inner intimacy, "eternally more intimate to me than I am to myself". We could summarize it as: "I am –the empirical self–outside of myself; not only is God within my interiority, he is my interiority, but from God comes the power which draws me back into myself, and so to God." From such a perspective, we observe the substantiality, the power and the necessity of focusing on the "true subject". Plato, largely at the origin of such a perspective in Western philosophy, even made up categories of soul, defining the quality of different men, divided between bronze, silver or golden souls, depending on the quality of this "subject", as we observe it in its daily thoughts and activities. A distinction that reminds us of the Chinese opposition between "little men" and "noble men". And for Zhuangzi as well, one could say that access to the Dao is the most intimate access to the self.

More pragmatically, in the empiricist Anglo-Saxon tradition, Locke stresses the importance of the memory as the crucial dynamic of self-consciousness: this faculty is what allows us to relate past experiences of events to the present, what makes us a "person". To be an individual, endowed with a subjectivity, means to remain conscious of one's own past and one's own present. He has to be able to think of himself as the author of all his past actions. Marx prefers to define the subject as a product of social and economic circumstances, a perspective which sort of deprives the "transcendental self" of its "privacy". For him: "It is not the consciousness of men that determines their existence, it is their social existence that determines their consciousness". For Nietzsche, the sovereignty of the subject is only an illusion. In fact, the senses and consciousness are the mere toys of an impersonal self, which is the master of the thoughts and feelings of the "I". For him, as for many linguists, the preeminence of the "I" is only a linguistic construction. In other words, the idea of the subject comes from an illusion created by language: the invention of the "I". He writes: "Something thinks, but to say that this something is precisely the ancient and famous I, that is to express with moderation a mere hypothesis, an assertion, and certainly not an immediate certainty." In fact, this "I" is not really a universal "self-enunciation". For example, in Japanese, one does not explicitly point the centrality of the subject towards oneself.

One important and traditional way to capture the idea of transcendent self, is the "soul". This concept is encountered in various cultures. Its symbolic forms or definitions are varied, throughout religious, philosophical, psychological or popular representations, including in Chinese culture. In Greek culture, the soul (psyche) originally refers to "blowing" or "breath", and can indicate "life", "spirit", "consciousness", in opposition to the body, to what is material (soma). In Latin, « anima » (breath, respiration), is the vital principle or spiritual principle, immanent or transcendent, of a living being. Its meaning oscillates between signifying the "life principle" of a living entity, its "intellectual principle", or being an actual "spirit", separable from the body. It can be attributed to a specific entity, object, plant, animal or human, to a given phenomenon, or to the totality of the universe. In vitalistic doctrines, considering that life is not reducible to matter, the soul can survive a material death and go "in the beyond" and be eternal. Animism is a doctrine that attributes a soul to practically everything. One of the most extensive analyses of the concept of soul is Aristotle's. For him, it is not a substance, but a "breath of life", which does not exist in itself, although all living beings need it: "The soul is the first act of an organized body", or it is the "form of the body". He distinguishes three types of soul. The vegetative soul, endowed with the faculty of nourishment, growth, and generation. The animal soul, endowed with an ability to feel and move. The intellective soul, endowed with a faculty of knowing, including reason, character, feeling, consciousness, memory, perception, etc.

In the Christian culture, inherited from the previous culture such as the Egyptian one, the soul becomes the moral or spiritual essence of the individual. As a separate entity, it will survive biological death, and will be evaluated at this "passing over" moment on its moral qualities, a judgment that will determine its future fate. For example, paradise and hell, each soul according to its merits, are such consequences of one's earlier life. The "karma" is a Hindu version of the afterlife, where the "self" will undergo consequences of its behavior and actions in subsequent lives, pleasant or suffering, although the ideal would be the interruption of the series of reincarnations, the Samsara, and attaining Nirvana, the oneness of all things. We see here a major opposition between the insistence on individual identity, and the disappearance of it, two opposite forms of ideal and world vision.

Chinese culture does as well have some concept of the soul to explain human existence, as a very ancient tradition. It is divided in Hun (cloudy soul) and Po (white soul). In this dualistic tradition, every living human has two souls. Hun is the spiritual soul, ethereal, yang, which leaves the body after death, a vital force expressed in consciousness and intelligence. Po is the corporeal soul, substantive, yin, expressed in bodily strength and movements, which remains with the corpse of the deceased. Although there will be some variants of this concept throughout history. Both Hun and Po need to be nourished by the essences of the cosmic vital forces in order to stay healthy, they are not totally separate from the totality. When a person dies, the Hun gradually disperses in heaven, and the po returns to earth. But if the concept of soul remains common in religious and popular culture, it is not so much the preoccupation as most philosophers such as

Confucius or Zhuangzi, for whom man's actions are better defined by their psychological, moral or cognitive character rather than by some specific entity.

Let us now examine what can represent for Zhuangzi the "transcendent self", as illustrated in this story by Shan Pao. We know that "he lived among the cliffs, drank only water, and did not go after gain like other people. He went along like that for seventy years and still had the complexion of a little child." What does it imply, in terms of his being and functioning? He lives on his own, therefore he is autonomous and does not depend on other persons, a key characteristic of the "transcendent self", in opposition to the heteronomous, outwardly determined empirical self, who is very relational. He drinks only water, therefore he is not looking for sensual pleasure and immediate gratification, he does not look for excitement through intoxication. As well, water symbolizes the idea of purity of the self, evoking the purity of the Dao. Then we learn that he did not pursue gain, unlike most people, as it is specified. Therefore, he is not corrupted, he is not greedy, since he is not looking for material possessions, which should make him more accessible to the Dao. Again, he is autonomous, he is free, since he does not pursue "external" things. And he is different, he is special, since most other humans are rather greedy. Lastly, we learn that in his old age, he still had the physical complexion of a child. Of course, we can take this description as a physical specification, the appearance of a man who lived a wholesome life, and therefore kept in good shape, remaining young and healthy. But knowing Zhuangzi, and within the given context, we suspect it is a metaphor for the spiritual life as well. The idea of "child" stands again for purity, but as well ingenuity, faith and trust, the state of being of a person not corrupted by sordid calculations. As well as his longevity, his advanced age was rather rare at the time, which reflects the good state of his being, physical and moral, two criteria that go together in the Chinese thinking. Overall, we can conclude that Shan Pao was a wise man, if not a saint, an example of virtue for all of us. To attain such a state, he had to resist all the usual temptations of the body and the mind, such as pleasure, wealth, fame and power. And since he seems to be isolated, he must have learned his wisdom by himself, which shows a great degree of freedom and autonomy. He is morally strong and authentic. He is self-reflexive, he had to think a lot about himself, about the world, and separate the essential from the secondary. His main preoccupation is to be the best person possible, rather than being successful through social recognition. His life must have been hard, since what is described is far from constituting an easy life, but this did not stop him. This whole description shows well the character and life of someone concerned with his "transcendent self", what can be called a "noble man".

We could expect Zhuangzi to promote such an ideal or image, which for many readers would correspond to the asceticism of the Daoist ideal, the glorification of a saint. But that would be disregarding the very nature of our author or his text. Zhuangzi recoils from any dogmatism, from any complacent self-satisfaction or from any established system. For him, everything, especially apparently serious matters, is an object for criticism and a target for laughter. Therefore, poor Shan Pao suffered his demise: "Unfortunately, he met a hungry tiger who killed him and ate him up". Of course, his healthy body could lawfully be quite appetizing for a tiger, and this end would be a rather natural, beautiful and ecological death! But the issue here is more of the order of a punchline, like in a joke, including the "unfortunately", that ironically tries to make the story sound so sad.

Thus, what can this tragic ending signify? The key is given by the sentence: "Both these men failed to give a lash to the stragglers".

Explained more conceptually would be to say: "they were punished by their own failure, by their own deficiencies". In the case of Shan Pao, it would mean that he was so focused on his internal reality that he forgot the external one. Just like for Chang Yi the demise had to do with his internal self, which he was forgetting. Of course, we admire Shan Pao for his sense of autonomy, but we must as well identify his incapacity to recognize and adapt to the principle of reality: reality is often "otherness", what does not belong to us, what comes from outside, that we ignore and largely do not control. The lesson is that the "transcendent self" is not omnipotent, it depends as well on the outside, it cannot avoid its own "outwardness", if only because the self-reflexive dimension of our being is incorporated in a physical being. The spirit cannot ignore material reality, it cannot deny its "otherness". From this derives the idea of mutual necessity of the apparent duality "inside – outside", which implies a dialectical relation between the subject and its environment. In opposition to Shan Pao, Chang Yi is too concerned with the outside, with his social success, and forgot he had an inside, did not take care of his own health, and died of an internal fever, much younger than Shan Pao. We can here identify a slight preference of Zhuangzi, since his text seems rather favorable to Shan Pao, to whom he granted a more extended longevity, although his punishment is rather cruel and violent: being eaten by a tiger. We can nevertheless conclude that he rather favors the transcendent self, while warning us against its abusive sense of omnipotence, the autistic tendency of this self, signaling its disconnection from reality. One cannot forget the Dao, the "principle of everything": relating to the Dao is what determines the value of the inner self, what provides it with its particular De, its individual power, which has to be grounded in the Dao in order to be adequate or real.

Lastly, one could address a formal criticism of our usage of the "transcendental self" concept in the context of the Zhuangzi. By simply stating that unlike in numerous western philosophers, there is no such expression here, or no mentioned equivalent. Let us answer here that there are two ways to examine the presence of a concept in a philosophical work, or even in literature: as an experience, consciously described, especially when identified as a recognized pattern, or as a name, formally used or coined. In the western tradition, the latter is largely privileged, a philosophical work is often a sort of "cathedral of concepts", since those abstract terms structure the writing. But in some other traditions, it is not necessarily the case, although a number of specialists will claim that for this reason it is not philosophy anymore. Such a position will most likely come to the conclusion that philosophy is hence reserved to the western world, generally originated or connected to the "Greek miracle", a rather common dogma. Anything else will be called "Wisdom", "Thinking", "Culture", or anything else. But if we accept that the nature of philosophy can be determined otherwise, through problematization, narration, metaphorical concepts, then we can identify philosophy and concepts in other forms or places. Our standpoint is that any significant phenomenon, with some universal potentiality, recurrently described in an identifiable way in a work, can be called a concept, even without a name. As well, we could oppose in this domain the "occidental way" and the "Chinese way" of philosophizing, or more generally of thinking. Although geographically and historically, the most common in the world is the "non occidental way". In the "occidental way", as we outlined, the concept is named, clearly defined, when the Chinese way is more allusive, often metaphorical, described rather than analyzed directly and explicitly. The background in such opposition is the difference between an "analytic" or "conceptual" language, and an "evocative" language. The Chinese idea, if we can say, does not have to "stick" exactly to its object, it just needs to "point" to it, to "evoke" it. This can be described as the difference between "saying by saying", and "saying without saying".

Then let us therefore propose the hypothesis that we can identify two ways by which Zhuangzi describes a "transcendental self": through a "unity of consciousness" and a "unity of action", two modalities than can be noticed in the work, which can be as well be designated as a concept of identity. Shan Pao and Chang Yi, who respectively represent "inner life" and "outer life". Thus, very often, in his narrations Zhuangzi presents some very marked characters, almost archetypal. We could call them "transcendent subjects", in the sense that the various words and actions of these personalities, or even their end, are determined by these identities, identities that we find in various manners, with which we could establish a categorization. In this sense, there seems to be a unity of the subject, in spite of transformations and apparent multiplicity. For example, between Zhuangzi and the butterfly, there are two ways of being, although through this "perspectivism", Zhuangzi invites us to "go beyond" these oppositions, to "transcend" them, in order to be part of the indeterminacy of the Dao.

As for consciousness, and its individual unity, without naming it, it seems that Zhuangzi invites us to envisage it. Even though this unity of consciousness becomes "unconscious", or rather "meta-conscious", as we see in the work of the butcher Ting or with the wheelwright. The author describes in those cases different registers of conscious activity, showing a progression taking place in a discontinuous way, but it leads or points toward a unity of consciousness, or rather a unity of being and action. The wooden rooster is an interesting illustration of this phenomenon as well, as strange as it appears, since this "fighting creature" is learning to be "numb", not reacting, to become impassive. The example of the butterfly helps us to understand this process, which we could characterize as leading to the "great awakening", some superior mental state which goes beyond different "little awakenings", a consciousness that transcends all different perspectives, or Dao. This is reminiscent of Spinoza's three levels of consciousness: first mere opinion or hearsay, then understanding cause and effect or rationality, finally the unity in God, the oneness of all things. There is a "transcendent self", although we are invited to go through or overcome those singular differences and identities in order to access it. This work of negativity makes the issue difficult for the reader. Since the unity of action becomes a non-action (wu wei), and the unity of consciousness becomes unconscious, as a passage to the Dao.

One of the difficulties with defining some kind of transcendental self in the Zhuangzi is the fact that such a concept has for him a dynamic and open perspective: individuals are considered as unique but changing beings. The unlimited Dao is viewed as the ultimate source for individuals to conform to, thus releasing individual mind from boundedness, into a realm of infinite openness and freedom. Basically, the "transcendent self" is "no-self". This has the significance of releasing the individual mind into a totally free and unconstrained realm of nothingness or emptiness, thus endorsing an infinite openness to any possible development of all individuals. Therefore, since there is no need for a persistent or determined attitude toward anything, since the individual spirit is conforming to the free, open, and dynamic Dao, one will keep an open, free, and flexible attitude toward one's own "completed mind" or already constructed "self." This "selfless self" does not prohibit, on the contrary, the self to constitute an integrated and complete entity, since in opposition to usual Chinese cultural tendencies, the Zhuangzian self can exist independently from other entities and from society: it is not the "incomplete part" of a "general whole", as in Ruist thinking. In this context we should mention the concept of Ziran, a word often translated in English as "nature," although the original meaning in ancient Chinese actually emphasizes the meaning of "self-initiated" or "spontaneous," as "zi" means "self," and "ran" means "as such." We should come back at a later point to this concept.

One last issue is the one of "forgetting one's self". It does not mean that the individual "self" has totally dissolved or disappeared, physically or mentally. We should notice there are two different "selves" in the sentence "Now I have lost myself", used by Zhuangzi. The first is the original and innate self, which is as free, open, and spontaneous as the Dao itself; the other is the socially constructed self, which is fixed, closed, and constrained by his or her worldly existence. What should be forgotten and lost is the latter, not the former. Otherwise, we would not be able to understand why in other places Zhuangzi mocks and denounces those worldly people for "having lost their selves in materials" and "looking for fame but having lost their self" In general, when Zhuangzi urges an individual to conform to Dao, inviting us to release the individual mind into a boundless free realm, where it will no longer be constrained by its artificially constructed "self" which he calls his own, let alone any other political, social, and cultural control and restrictions. On one side, the empirical self is flexible, but heteronomous and corrupted, since it is focused on something from "outside": it is externally motivated. On the other side, being autonomous, the tendency of the transcendent self, "inner centered", is to be autistic, rigid, unmovable and closed. That is the opposition that is drawn between transcendental and empirical self, an opposition Zhuangzi wants to overcome, without falling in either existential trap.

The middle

As a conclusion of this text, like a moral to the story, Zhuangzi invites us to place ourself in a sort of "middle". "Do not go in and hide; do not come out and shine; stand stock-still in the middle. He who can follow these three rules is sure to be called the finest." In other words, do not get stuck in your interiority, and do not become a prisoner of external phenomenon, find some "right path" between those two extremes. We encounter here a great classical regulatory ideal, the "center" or "in-betweenness", which should be carefully examined.

In Greek thought, we encounter this principle quite early in the Delphic Maxim, which was perpetuated in the tradition. Along with the "know thyself, thou will know the gods and the universe", was inscribed on the walls of the Apollo temple "Nothing in excess". It is differently named as the "golden mean", "golden middle way" or the "right balance", referring to the desirable middle between two extremes, one of excess and the other of deficiency, both being flawed in their own way. This principle was both a moral and practical ideal, but as well an attribute of beauty, or theoretical ideal, the word "theory" finding its Greek etymology in "seeing". In this context, we should mention that we encounter in Plato the juxtaposition or coincidence of three fundamental transcendental concepts: Truth, Good and Beauty, which all have to do with the "middle principle". Which is here very understandable, since in this absence of excess, in the idea of balance, we can perceive an idea of harmony, through symmetry and proportion. Truth, because the order of the world is well-proportioned, Good, because everything obtains what fits it, what it deserves, nothing more, nothing less. Any excess was contrary to these laws of the universe, transgressing those principles of being.

On the ethical level, "Beauty", the motor and object of love, was to be imitated and reproduced not only in one's life, but as well in the guidance of the city (politics), in education, and of course in art. Any failure to respect this principle in terms of excess was considered "hubris" (pride, arrogance, imperiousness, which was a punishable "sin", as we learn in the story of Icarus, who ignored his father's warnings and flew too high, with the consequences that we know. A famous utilization of this opposition between "proportion" and "excess" is provided in the Aristotelian conception of ethics, where for example courage is considered a virtue, that stands between cowardice, a deficiency of courage, an excessive fear, and recklessness or temerity, an excess of courage, where one displays a lack of care about danger, an overconfidence, a certain unconsciousness about the possible results of one's actions.

Since Aristotle, we speak of a "Right middle" not so much as a position situated at equal distance or in the middle of two extremes, but as an equilibrium between two problematic extremes, of an optimal intermediate position which, by avoiding both excess and defect, is supposed to define the "right", not a mediocre or average position, but an excellent, perfect, optimal position. In the Aristotelian definition of courage, courage is not the "exact middle", since it is in a sense closer to temerity than to cowardice. Thus, every wise man avoids the excess and the defect, searches for the right path "in-between" and gives his preference not in relation to the object, but in relation to the person making the judgment. This principle applies to our actions as to our passions, our feelings or emotions, to our decisions as to our attitudes.

We encounter the Middle Way as well in the teachings of Buddha (6th century BC), first of all as an ethical or psychological principal, as a path between the extremes of religious asceticism and worldly self-indulgence. The tradition regards this regulatory ideal to be the first teaching that the Buddha delivered after his awakening. In this

Sutra, the Buddha describes the Noble Eightfold Path as the middle way of moderation, between the extremes of sensual indulgence and self-mortification. On one side the common banal temptation of material or physical pleasure, the way of ordinary people, low and coarse, on the other side the "lofty" addiction to self-mortification, which is hard and painful. Both are considered addictive, unworthy and unprofitable. Avoiding both these extremes, the Middle Path provides the right perspective on reality, it gives knowledge, and it leads to calm, to insight, to enlightenment and to Nirvana. It is the Noble Eightfold path because it dispenses right understanding, right thought, right speech, right action, right livelihood, right effort, right mindfulness and right concentration. On a more ontological level, Buddhism promotes a conception of the Middle Way which stands between eternalism and annihilationism: things are neither self-evident objects, eternal and independent substances or forms, nor are they pure illusion, a nihilistic non-existence. This Middle way is accounted for through the idea of "dependent origination": a sort of mutual principle of causality, a dynamic and reflexive system of cause and effect, which describes the existence of all objects and phenomena as effects of each other: everything is both cause and effect, or condition. When one of the causal conditions changes or disappears, the resulting object or phenomena will also change or disappear, as will the objects or phenomena depending on the changing object or phenomena. In Mahayana Buddhism, Nagarjuna will be influential in developing the Middle Way (Madhyamaka) as an epistemology and an ontology, taking a position between metaphysical claims that things ultimately either exist or do not exist. "Everything exists: that is one extreme. Everything does not exist: that is a second extreme." All phenomena can be explained and conceived as "momentary aggregates", therefore something between being and not-being. He deconstructed many of the terms used to describe existing things, leading to an insight into "emptiness" (Sunyata) as the ultimate reality.

In the Chinese tradition, we encounter the concept of Zhongyong, literally "impartiality and invariability", which has been translated variously as Doctrine of the Mean, Constant Mean, Middle Way, or Middle Use. The concept is known to us as the title of a book of Zi Si, grandson and promoter of Confucius, but it referred to the very ancient tradition of the Zhou era, in particular the famous "Book of rites". Those opuses are core works of the Confucian canon. Just like in Aristotle, virtue is there considered as the middle between two extremes, a crucial idea in Confucianism and Chinese philosophy in general, where it is taught that excess is just as much a problem as deficiency. In the Analects, Confucius is quoted as saying: "The virtue embodied in the doctrine of the Mean is of the highest order. But it has long been rare among people." However, the Analects never expand on what this term means, Confucius simply warns us about our ignorance of those matters.

Nevertheless, here are some elements about The Doctrine of the Mean as taught in the tradition. The goal of the mean is to maintain balance and harmony by directing the mind to a state of constant equilibrium. The person who follows the mean is on a path of duty and must never leave it. As we can see, it is primarily an ethical principle, with social and political implications, presented with very concrete applications. For example, a superior person behaves according to his status in the world, but remains a cautious or gentle teacher, showing no contempt for his or her inferiors. As well, common men and women can carry the "mean" into their practices, making sure they do not exceed the natural order. The main modalities this doctrine is concerned with are: moderation, rectitude, objectivity, sincerity, honesty and propriety, traditional Chinese and confucianist guidelines. The ruling principle of the mean being that one should never act in excess of anything. We should mention that the Zi Si work is divided in three parts: The Axis, which deals with Metaphysics, The Process, which deals with politics, The perfect word, which deals with ethics, primarily sincerity. The metaphysical aspect deals with traditional Chinese cosmological and ontological views, connecting the cosmos with the human. What heaven has disposed and sealed is called the inborn nature. The realization of this nature is called the process. The clarification of this process is called education. In such a worldview, sincerity is a crucial concept, since it refers to the true nature of a being, which allows him to connect to other beings, including animals and objects, and therefore to the "nourishing powers of Heaven and Earth", connecting therefore to the entire cosmos. Some of the more recent criticisms of this doctrine concerns the permanent spirit of concession inspired by such a perspective. For example, Mao Zedong stated that such an attitude failed to realize that some situations or actions deserve absolute negation, denouncing the fact this type of compromise prevented China from progressing. It is an obstacle to dialectics as it stops qualitative change by emphasizing maintaining balance and harmony, excluding radical decisions. For Mao Zedong, critical of such "wisdom", without a radical proposal pushing it, Chinese society will not permit even the mildest reform.

We should mention in this context that the inspiration of such a criticism finds its origin in a different idea of the "middle", which comes from Hegel, and was later adopted and transformed by Marx. Hegel is not so interested in the concept of "middle" per se, but in the concept of mediation, the "action of middle", non-static, more conform to his dynamic vision of being and thought. The mediation is for him the third moment of dialectics, after thesis and antithesis, where the confrontation of opposites, in a dialogical way, can lead to a synthesis, which implies a qualitative transformation in the process, synonym of progress. It is not a matter of a peaceful "conciliation", "concession" or "in-betweenness", but the nonlinear emergence of some new reality within the confrontative undertaking of negativity, breaking away from the binary traditional approach to the "middle". For him, this "mediation" is an essential aspect of reality, perceived as a permanent process of negativity and replacement, cyclic or linear. In a way, just like anything can be thought in a permanent process of cause and effect, everything for Hegel is constituted in a permanent process of affirmation, negation and overcoming, which can imply that "mediation" is the very substance of being. We could claim that this "mediation" is more rational, less mystical than some "absolute" considered as the actual eternal "middle".

Lastly, on the western side, we should mention the peculiar vision of French philosopher Blaise Pascal, who dealt as well with the "middle" concept. He presents the "middle" as an undefined "in-between", which is both the reality of things and the right place to be. In a world divided between the "for" and "against", he is looking for the position that will overcome the opposites because it is equidistant from the extremes or overhangs them. But strangely, not for the reason of an ideal: he takes side with the "majority", in order to defend "mediocrity", a concept which finds its etymology in "medium". He therefore allies with common people, against the "half-wise", the "smart people" or scholars, who want to distinguish themselves. "Only mediocrity is good. To leave the middle is to leave humanity." His philosophy of "happy medium" recommends temperance between wisdom and insanity, a form of humility, reflecting our statute of humble sinner. One of his famous quotes, an apology of the middle is: "For after all what is man in nature? A nothing in relation to infinity, everything in relation to nothing, a central point between nothing and everything and infinitely far from understanding as well. The ends of things and their beginnings are relentlessly concealed from him in an impenetrable secret. He is equally incapable of seeing the nothingness out of which he was drawn and the infinite in which he is immersed." The pascalian vision is the one of a submissive and mediocre man, who could only grow by obedience and mysticism, and therefore should accept the reality of the middle.

In the Zhuangzi, the "middle" plays a very important role, and it has a specific name: the "pivot". It functions in a rather radical way, which somewhat resembles the process by which Nagarjuna uses it. Unlike many other ways to refer to a middle, nothing is predefined: any given presupposition would be an obstacle to this "middle", which remains therefore quite undefined. For this reason, it touches crucial ontological issues and problematizes any fixed paradigm. The following quote captures well his conception. "The wise man therefore, instead of trying to prove this or that point by logical disputation, sees all things in the light of direct intuition. He is not imprisoned by the limitations of the "I", for the viewpoint of direct intuition is that of both "I" and "Not-I." Hence, he sees that on both sides of every argument there is both right and wrong. And we should question not only statements and beliefs, but as well the "I" itself, the speaking subject, without denying its existence. He also sees that in the end they are reducible to the same thing, once they are related to the pivot of the Tao. Let us remind the reader in this context the indeterminate nature of the Dao, remaining therefore beyond opposites. Thus the "direct intuition" mentioned here does not connect or identify some type of evidence, but precisely a "non-evidence", some grounding and undefinable primary reality. Therefore neither "society" nor harmony" or any ethical principle are defined as grounding the thinking and behavior. On the contrary, any attempt to establish such grounding represents precisely the problem. A position which conforms with his skepticism toward morality that we have described previously, a specific criticism which represents only a particular case of the author's general suspicion toward any established dogma. If Zhuangzi, who does not totally reject reason, criticizes the "This is this and that is that", it is not to deny the reality of it, but to warn us against the illusion and abuse such distinctions or oppositions can entail. We end up believing those statements or theories, and we lose track of the Dao, the ultimate perspective we should keep focusing on. In guise of clarification, we can use the Buddhist distinction between conventional truth and absolute truth.

The fact that Zhuangzi choses the concept of "pivot" rather than the one of "middle" is important. It is to remind us of the dynamic nature of reality. The traditional Chinese concept of "harmony" easily leads us into some static perspective of "perfect nature", both for the cosmos and for society, as a sort of established balance. This is not necessarily the case, as we can see in the Yi King, which is all about processes, but Zhuangzi sees in the intellectual environment and usual practices a strong temptation to decree and enforce fixed rules for thinking and behavior. He reminds us about cycles, how opposites feed in each other. "Life is followed by death; death is followed by life. The possible becomes impossible; the impossible becomes possible. Right turns into wrong and wrong into right – the flow of life alters circumstances and thus things themselves are altered in their turn". All opposites "are reducible to the same thing, once they are related to the pivot of the Tao." When the wise man grasps this pivot, he is in the center of the circle, and there he stands while "Yes" and "No" pursue each other around the circumference⋯The pivot of Tao passes through the center where all affirmations and denials converge. He who grasps the pivot is at the still-point from which all movements and oppositions can be seen in their right relationship. Hence, he sees the limitless possibilities of both "Yes" and "No." Abandoning all thought of imposing a limit or taking sides, he rests in direct intuition. Therefore, I said: "Better to abandon disputation and seek the true light!"

We can observe in such a description a radically different conception of the middle: it is not situated anywhere in-between two opposites, it is "elsewhere": it cannot be defined by the interplay of opposites. In order to reach the pivot, we need to totally escape the pre-established opposition, until this point where the opposition seems vain and meaningless. Not only situated externally in relation to the opposites, but as well externally in relation to the opposition itself, and even externally to the paradigms sustaining the opposition, be it the very principle of contradiction. Each pair of opposites is merely an occasion to reach the center of all, the pivot which grants "reality" and "unreality" to everything. This reminds us the Nagarjuna principle formalized in this fashion: when we encounter an opposition between A and B, the truth does not reside in A, nor does it reside in B, nor does it reside in A and B, nor does it reside in neither A nor B, but it resides elsewhere. This scheme is actually supposed to lead us to the unconditional, the same way Zhuangzi wants to lead us to the pivot of the Dao, the absolute center of all things. This somewhat reminds us of God as defined in his famous sentence by the mysterious author from antiquity Hermes Trismegistus: "God is an infinite sphere, the center of which is everywhere, the circumference nowhere." Such a theme will be picked up in the tradition, in different ways, for example by Nicholas of Cusa or Spinoza. The general idea is that things have to be thought adequately in the perspective of the indeterminate transcendence, God, which is the center of all things, the absolute which alone is the unconditioned metric and matrix. To wit the Dao, which is mysterious, unbounded and in a way centered everywhere. And just like the reality of all things can only be seized in the godhead, the adequate reality of all things can only be perceived in the Dao.

Let us now go back to our story for a moment. Both "heroes" are being criticized in the way they lead their life, and comparing them to shepherds, they are accused of failing to "watch for stragglers and whips them up.'" By the way a very different attitude to the "soft caring" approach of Christ toward the "lost lamb". One has to be harsh with one's own failings, since it is our precious life we are dealing with. The ironic touch on this story is that in this story, it is Confucius speaking, most likely reinvented by Zhuangzi. Although what he says in this context makes sense, since the present "middle" has to do with human behavior, the specialty of the old Master. The ideal he proposes, "stand stock-still in the middle", as stuck and motionless as a trunk, would be precisely what Zhuangzi would criticize in the Ruist ethics, formal and serious, where principles are totally fixed. With of course the "guarantee of a good reputation", a very traditional Chinese preoccupation, being "sure to be called the finest"; this captures the suspicion of Zhuangzi about the motivation behind most of the "good behavior" in Ruism: to be recognized. In opposition to the "middle" of Confucius, very determined and rigid, the "middle" of his critic is not known, it is undetermined. All we know is that it has nothing to do with what is already described. Neither one of the opposites, neither their in-between, but elsewhere.

Let us take a concrete example of this displacement of the middle. In numerous traditions, be it Aristotelian or Confucian, temperance and moderation are recommended. They represent the wisdom of the middle path, a form of prudence that appeals to common sense as the best way to act. Within it, as a sort of untold or told paradigm, there is contained the idea of "healthy relations", and the concept of efficiency that comes with it, since good relations to others allow us to pursue and obtain our goal: no one should be hurt, people should feel good about us, as much as possible, so we can obtain what we want. Respect others, you will be respected: it is all about give and take; behind the moral varnish, there is very pragmatic consideration. If the absolute is the center, God, Dao or else, all these practical or moral considerations become side issues, trivial, insignificant. What respect is there to be earned in most petty human endeavors, no matter how noble they are? But of course, such an attitude seems hubristic, placing oneself above others, an attitude considered intolerable by those who take to heart common human considerations, goals and preoccupations. One characteristic of such an attitude is what the Greeks called parrhesia: the capacity to say the truth, without any consideration for the sensitivity or receptivity of "others". Truth is the issue, truth is the center, anything else is redundant, shallow and insignificant. And in this sense, Zhuangzi, concerned with truth, views the Dao as the center, since "The pivot of Tao passes through the center where all affirmations and denials converge." In this middle, nothing is right or wrong, nothing is opposed. This reminds us of the non-aliud (not-other) of Nicholas of Cusa, which he uses to define God. Everything "that is" is other than something, except God which is "not-other".

Let us take here another idea of the author. Zhuangzi, who enjoys conceptual metaphors, uses in a passage: the analogy of the "ring". And he writes: "With the pivot, only then is the middle of the ring attained, and because of this, thinking is no longer impoverished". But the middle of the ring is outside of the ring, and at the same time inside the ring, a strange paradoxical inside and outside. After all, one can claim that in a way the finger is inside the ring, the same way that we claim we are "inside a tunnel". A ring is nothing but a small and short tunnel which cannot contain the whole finger, therefore the finger is not inside the ring, since not contained. The main point is that the middle is "outside" in some way: the middle is a "non-something", a principle dear to Zhuangzi, applied to different concepts, such as the non-action (wuwei). It can be said that for this reason, because of its non-materiality and its situation in emptiness, the center of the ring has no real existence. At the same time, we have to recognize that without this middle, the ring would not exist, since it is constitutive of the very existence of the ring. Both for conceptual reasons, since there is no circle without a center, but as well for material and genetic reasons, since the person that made this ring most likely needed to start with the establishment of a center around which to make the circle of this ring. Not realizing or thinking this problem "impoverishes the thinking", since we are not conscious of the very nature of a ring, as a circle. We are "stuck" in the object, "becoming an object for the object", instead of freeing ourself by "going back to the origin of things", as he writes as well. In other words, using more recent formulations, he invites us to think about the conditions of possibility of the existence of this ring. We should add in this context that as a parallel to the purely epistemological or ontological implications, we can envisage the psychological ones. Since a ring represents in Chinese culture a symbol of wealth, the person who only sees the object and is obsessed with it, obsessed with the possession of it, actual or virtual, stops thinking this thing and "becomes a thing", therefore "impoverishing his thinking". Therefore the "rich" is actually "poor", since he is not free from greed, a recurrent Zhuangzian theme. The pivot, this dynamic center, the substantial ontological middle, is the vanishing point around which adequate knowledge can be acquired. This pivot is "other" from a material standpoint, logical standpoint, psychological standpoint, ontological standpoint, etc.

From this standpoint, we can address the critique made to Zhuangzi of being a skeptic. Indeed, he does not accept any particular position, and whatever the statement, he is critical of it, since you cannot say categorically "this is this" or "this is not that", the foundation of any assertion. But it is not because it is radically false, the problem rather being that we give too much value to our words, we get too attached to such statements. We do not set them in the adequate perspective, conditioned within a given paradigm, we do not remain conscious of the limitedness of such a paradigm. At the same time, there is an absolute, an unconditional, the problem being the relative indeterminateness of this "grounding". This somewhat resembles Plato's dialectics, where we slowly have to move upwards from different levels of hypothesis in order to reach an unhypothetical first principle, the highest form of knowledge, rather undetermined. The "unhypothetical" is both a necessary condition and it cannot be formulated, two characteristics that oppose it to the "hypothetical". This unhypothetical is ontologically a starting point, but as the product of a thought process, it is to be introduced as an ultimate premise. At the same time, to determine the nature of those unhypothetical principles is a rather obscure endeavor. It starts resembling a leap of faith, although reason points toward it. The image of the "sun" in the "Allegory of the cave" of Plato, as the source of truth, shows the paradox: the more it is luminous, the more enlightening it is, the more invisible it is, since it blinds us.

There is another way to understand the harsh criticism Zhuangzi makes to squabbles between philosophical schools and opposite thoughts, that relates to his pivot concept. Statements or theories should not be taken as certainties, we should not "believe" in them, not cling to them. They are the mere production of general schemes, of established paradigms. And those paradigms, in his perspectivist outlook, are just different ways to look at a given phenomenon. Those opposites or differences should not be qualified as "true or false", but observed the way we can observe different sides of a reality. This does not prohibit certain philosophical preferences, as we have seen in our analysis on "perspectivism", but we have to keep in mind and accept the diversity of perspectives as a crucial dimension of reality. From the standpoint of the "pivot", we can observe with a certain distance the multifaceted, kaleidoscopic nature of things, keeping in mind the "groundless grounding" of the knowable world. Everything "rotates around" the Dao, everything comes from it and interplay under its "mysterious" influence. The Dao in that sense is both "middle" and "medium", the latter being the "substance" within which everything is happening, which provides substantiality and understandability to all phenomena. Within such a framework, it becomes meaningless to determine the "right and wrong" between opposite theses. One has to simply see how they relate to each other and what they imply, from the standpoint of the inevitable and substantial middle.

Finitude

Let us now conclude our analysis of this passage by examining the existential dimension of this story, through the concept of finitude, that seems to capture rather well the present idea of Zhuangzi. Finitude is the quality or state of being finite or limited. It characterizes what is finite, the character of everything that has a limit in some respect. This finiteness or limit is of different types: temporal, spatial, conditional, structural, etc. For the human being, whose existence is limited by death, finitude is understood principally in relation to time. It is therefore a trait, even a definition, of his essentially mortal condition. But this mortality does not exhaust the concept of finitude. Finitude refers as well to our imperfection, our fragility, our impotence, our ignorance, our different types of weaknesses, physical, psychological, social, etc.

The philosophy of finitude, represented by postmodernity, maintains that our finite experience of life is the ultimate horizon of human knowledge. There is no absolute truth, thinking the absolute is pretentious, we have no access to such a concept. So it is with objectivity or certitude. We have no grounds for claiming that a determinate reality is what it is, whether it is God, myself or the world. The recognition that we are finite and limited, destitute beings arbitrarily "thrown" in the world, into a particular time and place, discredits all discourses that claim access to ultimate truth. We can only remain as a kind of stranger to the world. Although, as phenomenology claims it, the perspective can be reversed, and finitude can become a positive determination of our existence, what establishes its contour, giving us a clear existential determination. As well, the consciousness we have of our finitude and our precarious condition is an essential aspect of our existence: the perception of our inevitable physical degradation, the fragility of our being, grants value to our existence. This "upgrading" of our finite self is well captured through Blaise Pascal's idea of "dignity": "Man is great in that he knows himself to be miserable".

What is the manifestation of finitude for Zhuangzi in this story? One should look at those little anecdotes of the Zhuangzi as minute theatrical opus, capturing some essential issues in an intensely condensed way, in an innocuous and tame way, going easily unnoticed. Let us examine the introductory part of the present narration. The Duke Wei, like often aristocrats in the Zhuangzi, is concerned with knowledge and learning. Of course, ironically, he represents the shallow dimension of "culture", greedy, formal and superficial. Thus, he wants to learn a life lesson from Chu Hsien, visibly a master in such art, a wise man. He asks Tien Kai-chih, whom he calls "friend" of the master, probably to flatter him, since we learn that he is "just" the gardener. Flattery is a recurrent target of Zhuangzi, for different reasons. First of all, it is a sort of moral obligation in the traditional social code, honoring the "other", where it is called "respect". Second, because it means lying to the other person, in order for him to feel "good" or "important", instead of telling him the truth. Third, it is a manipulative form of speech, since it is generally produced in order to "obtain" something from the other person, minimally a similar type of flattering speech, if not more. The "dramatic" or "comic" dimension of this exchange, quite Zhuangzian, is the fact that the aristocratic and powerful man, the Duke, is asking the "lowly" gardener for some "advice", a perspective that does not fit the culture.

To this "fake" speech, the answer of Tien Kai-chih is of a double nature. First of all, he does not accept the "lie", by humbly stating he is a mere "gardener", dealing with a broom rather than with "great" ideas. Second, he puts forward his "existence" rather than a "speech", no matter how deep the speech could be. He even exclaims himself, rather surprised that he would have "heard" anything from the Master, being a "mere" gardener. Of course, he is being ironic, since we discover later that he has learned something, which will be the "lesson" of the day. But he first makes the point that he will not enter in the social games, stating that he speaks as a gardener, not as a friend of the "great Master". Second, he makes a clear-cut distinction between the reality of existence and the "wise" discourse about life, giving priority to the former. Without saying it, the lesson has already started. He invites the Duke to quit playing these silly phony games, and to realize that a speech is merely a speech, when existence is primary.

The concept of finitude is introduced here as the realization of the limits of our life, the determination of our identity and function, which is what it is: speech cannot make it more than what it is. Speech can invent some type of "reality", but that "reality" is rather fictitious and external to our existence: it cannot really modify it. The Duke does not seem to quite understand the answer he received, but he insists, he wants to know, instead of understanding what is said. This scheme is a classic of avidity –for power, wealth and even knowledge: we see only what we want, not what we have. An avidity that prohibits us to be in the Dao, according to Zhuangzi. As well, the Duke tells Tien Kai-chih "do not be modest", he can only come up with a moral explanation of the answer, not an existential one, confirming the suspicion we had of his paradigm.

But Tien Kai-chih is generous and patient, he consents to the request of the Duke. He could pursue the hard way, although we can understand that it is hard to refuse a request from the power in place. So he gives him a quote from the Master, although a rather cryptic one, annoying for the listener. "He who is good at nourishing life is like a herder of sheep: he watches for stragglers and whips them up." The Duke has to think, rather than passively get a good recipe or a wise recommendation. So of course, he asks for an explanation, rather than trying to give an interpretation of his own.

Let us try to comply with his request and produce an explanation of this metaphor. First of all, life is not just a given, life is alive, it has to be nourished, and each one of us has to respond to such a necessity. In this sense, life is a responsibility, as Sartre would say, therefore something has to be done about it. It is not something we passively undergo: something has to be done for life to maintain itself. And of course, life is not here merely a biological phenomenon, but it is existence, what we, humans, construct throughout the years. Sartre would add that this existence determines our essence, who we are, and there lies the freedom of our self-determination. But to nourish life is like tending sheep: we have to watch them, to take care of them. And one of the main problems of tending sheep, according to this metaphor, is to "watch for stragglers". Now, a straggler is a person or an animal that is among the last or the slowest in a group to do something, for example, to finish a race, to come or to leave a place. Therefore, it refers to something missing, to some kind of inefficiency, to a deficiency, a lack, a weakness. Hence the concept of finitude. Of course, if we care, we have to remain aware, to watch and be conscious of the situation. But Zhuangzi does not simply invite us to watch out for those "stragglers", but to "whip them up". This recommendation is quite interesting, in particular for those who view Daoist philosophy or Zhuangzi as recommending some contemplative passivity, simply going with the flow, admiring the course of the sun in the heavens. There is a dynamic dimension of existence, action is necessary, sometimes we have to even proceed violently, for those who view Zhuangzi as some kind of flowery pacifist. In other words, we have to be conscious of our own finitude, but as well act upon it, to the extent possible, in order to nourish our own existence.

Then, as examples of this problem, the author describes two opposed characters: Chang Yi who is outwardly determined, and Shan Pao, who is internally determined. We already have been through some analysis of their respective character, let us look now at the implication from the general standpoint of existence. We would like at this point to propose the concept of "curvature of being". Each entity, object, animal or human has a certain way to be, a certain way to interact with the universe, to interact with other entities. And this interaction is more or less slanted, more or less outward or inward, more or less powerful: that is the way this entity is, in relation to what it is not. Thus it is with the two characters of the story as anyone else. This "way to be" has a certain manner and function, a certain nature, with its strengths and weaknesses. As a general principle, entities have the weaknesses of their strength, and the strength of their weaknesses.

Therefore, Chang Yi who was strong on the outside, got a "sickness that attacked him from the inside", and Shan Pao, who had a strong inside, got killed by the outside: a tiger ate him. That is the concept of finitude, expressed through the brief narration of two persons, in a brief way. Zhuangzi tells us we all have a way to be, maybe some ways are better than others, but still, we all have limits, and those limits are both who we are and the sign of our demise. Therefore, we should remain conscious of those limits, and work on them as much as possible. But for this, we have to look at ourself from the outside, as the shepherd looks at his sheep, and confront this limit. But in order to do this, we have to keep in mind the middle, the pivot, this indefinite central perspective which gives us the right measure about the finiteness of our own particular existence, and everyone else's. For Zhuangzi, the existential dimension is not separable from the ontological dimension. The finite has to be kept in relation to the infinite. Our life has to be thought through and lived in relation to the Dao, otherwise we lose the right perspective, and we become victim of ourself.

Comprehension questions

1. Why does the Duke question Tien Kai-chih?

2. Why does Tien Kai-chih decline to answer?

3. Why does the Duke doubt what Tien Kai-chih says?

4. What does the character of the shepherd represent?

5. Why is Tien Kai-chih using a story to answer the duke?

6. What does Shan Pao represent?

7. What does Chang Yi represent?

8. What are the problems with both types of life?

9. Why do the two characters die?

10. What is the ideal that Confucius proposes?

Reflection questions

1. Should we privilege the inner self or the outer self?

2. Can we control our own life?

3. Do we have to be master of ourselves?

4. Why are there tensions between the empirical self and the transcendental self?

5. Do we need a goal to lead a good life?

6. Should we give in to our desires?

7. Can we escape our environment?

8. How are human beings both active and passive?

9. Why are we subject to bad faith?

10. How is the "I" an illusion?

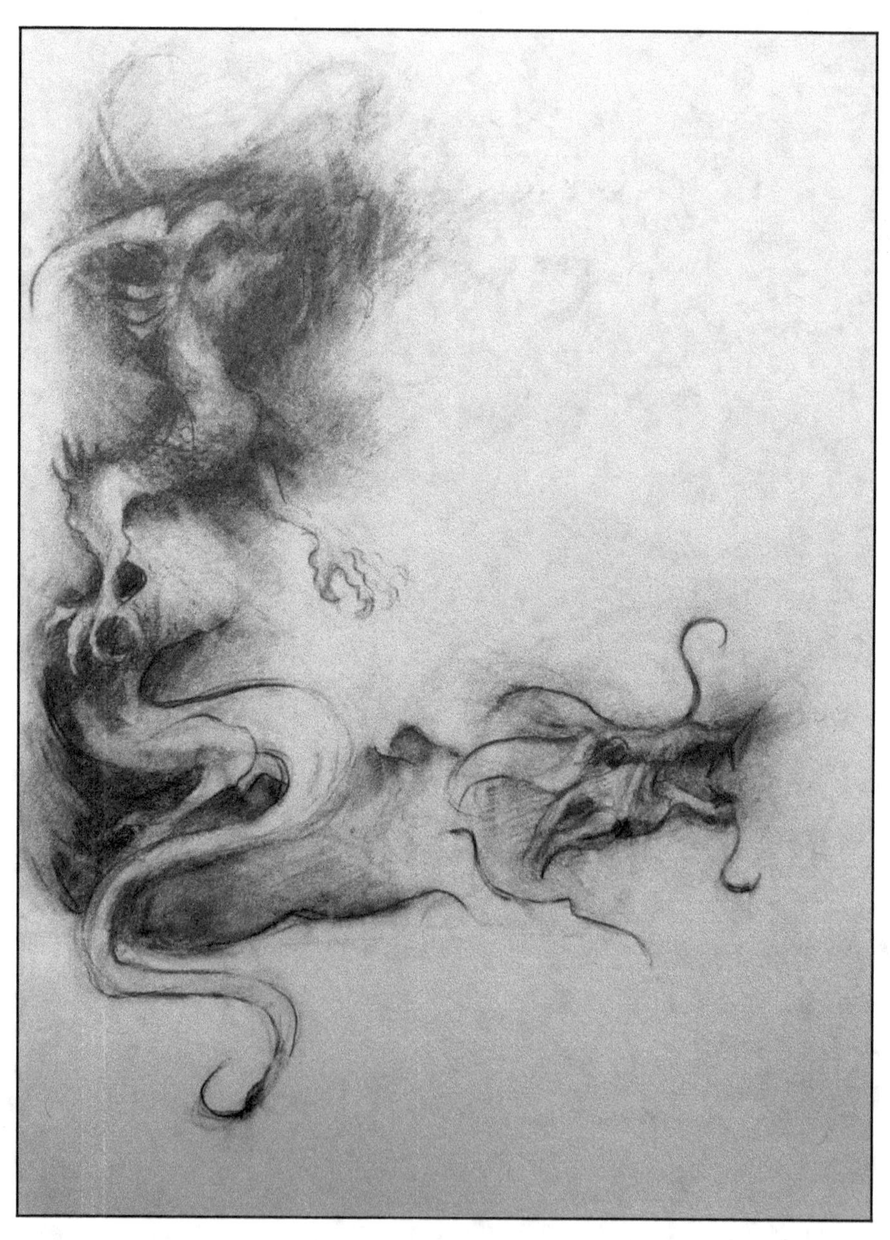

The encounter

Confucius called on Lao Tzu and spoke to him about benevolence and righteousness. Lao Tzu said: When chaff from winnowing blinds the eyes, heaven and earth and the four directions change places; when mosquitoes or horseflies sting the skin, the whole night you can't get to sleep. When benevolence and righteousness confusedly torment our hearts, no disorder is greater. To keep the world from losing its simplicity, just move as the wind pushes you and take your stand in the culmination of your virtuosity. Why all this hullabaloo, like one who shoulders and bangs a drum to search for a lost child? The snow goose stays white without a daily bath; the crow stays black without a daily inking. The simplicity of black and white isn't enough to debate over; the spectacle of fame and praise isn't enough to count as great. When the spring dries up, the fishes dwell together with each other on land, spitting moisture on each other and dampening each other with the froth, but it would be far better for them to forget each other in rivers and lakes. When Confucius returned from his visit with Lao Tseu, he did not speak for three days. His disciples said: "Master, you've seen Lao Tseu, what estimation would you make of him?" Confucius said: "At last I may say that I have seen a dragon, a dragon that coils to show his body at its best, that sprawls out to display his patterns at their best, riding on the breath of the clouds, feeding on the yin and yang. My mouth fell open and I couldn't close it; my tongue flew up and I couldn't even stammer. How could I possibly make any estimation of Lao Tseu!" This story has the form of a story, but more than a narration, it is the occasion for Zhuangzi to expose his thinking, contextually. The obvious theatrical staging of a crucial philosophical debate, the Copernican revolution of Daoism against traditional Chinese culture, an intellectual "mise en scène"structured around some invented encounter between Confucius, who represents mainstream thinking, although enlightened, and Lao-tse, the acknowledged founder of Daoist philosophy. Let us remind the reader that the presentation of Confucius by Zhuangzi is multifarious: sometimes laudative, sometimes ambiguous, but in this case, the Master incarnates the well-meaning but "dumb"student, literally "dumbfounded", as the end of the story tells us. This dialogue therefore presents to us the key elements of the opposition between Confucianist "human morality"and "Dao morality". As a conclusion, Confucius confesses to his students the awe provoked by Lao-Tse, described as a dragon, the key symbol of potency, used in general for the emperor. In this case, through a short speech, the dragon has precisely displayed his potency, his anchorage in both heaven and earth, his connection to the most fundamental metaphysical principles. This man, his speech, is so much above everything that he cannot even be "estimated", since he is beyond any measure, beyond usual "metrics".

Focusing

Focusing is an important concept in Daoist philosophy. That is one of the reasons behind the ulterior development of the meditation practice in that cultural context. But there are two main types of obstacles, which impede or paralyze the focusing process. External events and internal processes. Although the way Zhuangzi writes, it is never so clear if he addresses external physical events, described literally, or if he refers metaphorically to psychological processes. Since he does not care to specify his thinking, as the ambiguity is not for him a hindrance or a problem, quite the contrary. The mind must be able to function simultaneously on different levels. Although, paradoxically, it must be able to focus in order to do that, in order to be able to think different levels at the same time, in a dialectical way.

"When chaff from winnowing blinds the eyes". Winnowing is an activity periodically mentioned by Zhuangzi. We can find different reasons for this. The first, more practical, is that the culture of cereals is an important component of agricultural production, as a means of nourishment, therefore many persons will understand the reference to winnowing, and the experience it represents, since most of the population was agrarian at the time. Second, more spiritual, is that winnowing symbolizes an important mental activity: to separate and sort out the good and the bad, the useful and the useless. This action is central in the process of judgment, a preoccupation dear to this author. Let us not forget that the expression "critique, criticism", as in critical thinking, comes from a Greek verb krinein, which means to separate, to judge, to decide. Third, in this process of "purification", as Plato calls it, Zhuangzi is concerned with the consequence: besides the production of "good material" there is as well the production of "bad material", the engendering of a useless byproduct that is not without consequence. Indeed, it "blinds the eyes, heaven and earth and the four directions change places". Within the given context, it means to be totally lost, the absence of any significant landmark, since heaven, earth and the four directions constitute the matrix within which we can locate ourselves and anything else. And if those landmarks "change places", nothing is stable anymore, no spatial structure is reliable any more. In other words, this chaff makes us go crazy, it is alienating. An alienation which is produced by our own activity, no matter how necessary this activity is.

Next item: "when mosquitoes or horseflies sting the skin, the whole night you can't get to sleep". In this second metaphor, Zhuangzi addresses another theme dear to his heart: the tranquillity of the mind. Once again, we start with something which is useful and necessary: in this case, sense perception. But the cause of the problem is purely external: the aggression by insects, stimulating in an abusive way this sense perception, making us victims of the external world. This stinging affects us so much that we have no access to a peaceful mind, and therefore no access to the necessary rest of both body and mind. In the previous item, we had a more cognitive problem, the loss of stable landmarks. Here we have a more psychological or physiological issue: the absence of peacefulness, necessary for intellectual capacities, for adequate action, for existential wellbeing. Focusing takes on therefore a broader perspective.

The next item is much more problematic for the modern reader, harder to understand, although we have already somewhat started discussing it in the previous story: "when benevolence and righteousness confusedly torment our hearts, no disorder is greater". Although probably this is as well difficult to understand and to accept for Zhuangzi' s fellow-citizen, bathing in a traditional or confucianist environment where benevolence and righteousness were considered fundamental values. Let us try to enlighten the perplex reader with some of the reasons why the author engages in such a counter-intuitive criticism of rather universally accepted values. The main idea is that those confucianist cardinal virtues, benevolence, equity, righteousness are human productions, and their influence inhibits the pursuit of the true virtue: the Dao, endowed with a mysterious, more substantial, more fundamental influence. Only the Dao can harmonize the world. "Great Benevolence is not benevolent", writes Zhuangzi. Or "If benevolence has a constant object, it cannot be universal". The idea is that benevolence in general fixates on someone, on something particular, so it loses a wider perspective, more universal. The object of our benevolence is the fluidity of the Dao, not the fixation on a particular object. But of course, this wider perspective is harder to keep in mind, and it is outside of our immediate control. We cannot check its "benefits", and we cannot even expect tangible results, especially the recognition for our actions, the gratitude from our neighbor that we are so much fond of. It is an attitude we have to maintain, where we seed without expecting to reap. Maintaining the right attitude is in itself our own reward, a rather demanding existential or psychological posture, although much more free. As well, Zhuangzi criticizes the "holier than thou"posture benevolence brings about. When one forces others "to listen to sermons on benevolence and righteousness, measures and standards, using other men's bad points to parade your own excellence". More "mysteriously"he describes a person who "held on to benevolence and worked to win men over. He won men over all right, but he never got out into the realm of not-man."This not-man representing some type of "overman", in opposition to petty man. For him, those moral characteristics are not part of "man's true form", they make us worry too much, they produce lots of useless fuss and hubbub in the world. "They are intended to comfort the hearts of men, but in fact destroy their natural constancy."It alters the peace of mind rooted in the connection to the Dao. Thus the accusation of disorder and torment formulated against benevolence, since we don't focus on the appropriate level of reality.

Simplicity

"To keep the world from losing its simplicity, just move as the wind pushes you and takes your stand in the culmination of your virtuosity."The concept of simplicity is fundamental in Daoist thinking, easily connected to the idea of "focusing", as the reader will intuit. Complication, complexity, entering in detail, circumstances, explanations will necessarily make us lose the central point, the essence, the heart or the core of the matter. A common mistake or confusion produced in everyday life or usual discussions is to amalgamate a fact or phenomenon with its cause, its conditions, its context or its consequences, just like if all this was the same object of reflection. Of course, those different elements can be connected, but a hasty unconscious mental gesture is to coalesce them as indissociable elements. It would be like saying that "Mary and Peter are one and the same because they are married". One famous sentence of Zhuangzi related to this problem is called "the illumination of the obvious". A sort of equivalent of the colloquial "what you see is what you get". Or described in a more refined way the experience of phenomenological reduction. To be conscious of what we perceive, independently or separated from our knowledge, our taste and desires, an objective perception deprived as much a possible from any subjectivity, although the "information"gathered is still our perception. It has to do with the ancient Greek Epoché: a "suspension of judgment", or a "withholding of assent", a term largely used among the various schools of Hellenistic Philosophy. To see what we see, without taking into account any other considerations. Lastly, we can recall here the warning of Aristotle, inviting us to distinguish the essential and the accidental: to separate in our thinking what pertains to the essence of the matter, the "what is", from any surrounding secondary information.

But let us now examine the simplicity as it is presented in the present sentence. "To keep the world from losing its simplicity, just move as the wind pushes you and take your stand in the culmination of your virtuosity." The boldness of the introductory clause is to be noticed. Since the simplicity is not simply regarding the thinking subject, the individual, but the totality of the world. For like in Plato and other such traditions, the mind, the thinking produces reality: words don' t just evoke reality, they engender it. In other words, one determines the nature of the world, one makes the world complicated or simple: it is not a given, it is generated. It is not in fact the world which is complicated or simple, but the mind that makes it complicated or simple. At the same time, in a paradoxical way, the author speaks about "the world losing its simplicity", a statement which implies that the original nature of the world would be a simple one, although the mind has the power to let it remain simple, or to vitiate, pervert or spoil this originary simplicity. Let us remind the reader that this simplicity can here refer either to the original chaos, Hundun, mother of all things, or to the Dao, the way by which all things operate. A reality that one can forget or deny, a suppression that bears actual consequences on the nature of the world itself, since our conscience and thinking produces reality.

Thus, in order to preserve this native simplicity, one should "just move as the wind pushes you". Now, what is the alternative or opposite to such a way of being? Since after all, when a directive is given, it must necessarily be because the "normal"or "natural"way of being goes against such a recommendation. Here, as common sense tells us, the most usual way to behave is to resist to the wind. For two reasons. The first one is that in general we are animated by "intentions", as Zhuangzi calls it. We want something, we have plans, desires, purposes, wills, therefore we are moved internally through a determinate path, that most likely does not fit the "path"or the "way"the wind is pushing us. It would be quite an amazing coincidence, although the sailboat is a sort of exception to this rule, which should know how to "go with the wind". But the use of the wind is already incorporated in its own functioning, as a driving force. In general, we consider the power of the wind as alienating: its power comes from outside, it does not concern us, and therefore it is against us when it imposes itself on our being. The second reason why we tend to resist to the wind is that it seems arbitrary, its power seems random, without any perceivable reason, and in general human beings do not appreciate the sense of arbitrariness, except of course when this arbitrary comes from themselves. Their own arbitrary not only is rather acceptable, but it is even welcome, praised as source of pleasure, freedom and pride.

How does this resistance to the wind complicate things? Well, we all had the experience of guests that we invited for dinner, and instead of just eating what they are given, and enjoy it, they complain about the food, in which there is too much of this or not enough of that, or they want some of this and not some of that, or they downright want something else to eat rather than what is in their plate. We can call those people fussy, or complicated, and we recoil from preparing food for them. So it is with the Dao. The universe follows its course, immense, eternal and unfathomable, but instead of accepting this supreme order, going along with it, enjoying it, we to go against it, to stop it, to determine our own course. A bit like the Chinese proverbial expression about "the mantis who tried to stop the chariot", referring to someone overrating himself, trying to hold back an overwhelmingly superior force; a sort of Chinese practical hybris. And that is where we lack simplicity and complicate things: life becomes much more difficult, more worrisome, since we don't know how to abandon ourselves.

At this point, we could conclude that the author invites us to a kind of complacent fatalism, a total self-abandon, but the sentence goes on, with the strange expression: "take your stand in the culmination of your virtuosity", an injunction which seems rather contradictory with the recommendation made in the previous part of the sentence. "Taking a stand", "one's virtuosity", both expressions seem rather incongruous with the idea of "moving as the wind pushes you". Although this is the same problem that we meet with the wu wei, this non-action that is still an action. Because indeed, in the paradoxical Daoist thinking, true power is not exerted by following a pretended personal and independent course of action, but through interaction with reality, through interplaying with natural processes. Therefore one is not a "victim" of the world, a puppet of the outside forces, since one maximizes his own power by making the best usage possible of reality. Circumstances therefore become our ally, rather than an enemy with whom we have to fight against, and it is in that sense that there is simplicity, an absence of complication. We espouse natural processes, rather than creating complicated strategies. An attitude which indeed exerts our power, our virtuosity, our "De", since it demands to be master of oneself, not to be driven by blind desire or greed, and to have this flexibility of mind that allows us to cope with reality in a harmonious way.

Efficiency

"Why all this hullabaloo, like one who shoulders and bangs a drum to search for a lost child?" One could immediately criticize such a statement, by claiming that beating the drum can alert the child, and attract him to the source of this noise, an acceptable strategy for finding the lost child. But let us for now credit the author and try to understand his idea from within, as an intention. By doing this, we will connect the present analysis to the previous concept, the one of simplicity, with its criticism of complication. The idea that is under attack in this question is the one of noise, which has a strong symbolic component. Let us examine it. Noise is unpleasant. It is a sound that does not fit any harmony. Words fit the harmony of reason. Notes fit the harmony of music. Noise is chaos. It has no structure, no meaning, no ordering, although we can sometimes notice some repetition in the noise, and it can be identified as the effect of a cause. Noise signifies something bad. Noise is generally the symptom of a problem: a fight, expressing pain, a mechanical defect, some uncontrolled process, etc. Noise is inefficient. In general, noise indicates a process that does not function the way it should. Noise instead of speech, when one cannot speak well, noise as shock between parts that do not fit well, etc. As well, the term "hullabaloo" indicates a loud noise, most likely made by people who are bothered and excited about something unpleasant. Their own unpleasant noise echoes the unpleasantness of the phenomenon that disturbs them. They are victims, and their distress is heard in the expression of their excessive emotion. As we saw in the "Wooden rooster" story, and elsewhere in Zhuangzi, excessive emotions are sign of greed, excess intentions, uncontrolled self, all of which engender a reactive type of behavior, neither calm, nor free, nor efficient.

The physical noise of "drum banging" and the psychological (physical as well) noise of the "hullabaloo" convey the same kind of chaotic qualities, radically estranged from the Dao. In opposition to this noisy and inefficient process, we are presented with natural processes that take place peacefully and naturally, meaning in accordance with the Dao. "The snow goose stays white without a daily bath; the crow stays black without a daily inking." The color of the birds (black or white) not only is a given, but it remains constant, in spite of any event, in spite of the circumstances. The reality of these birds takes place by itself, invariably. In this sense, they are not reactive, since nothing affects them. At first, the reader can be rather puzzled by such a comparison between a needed or desired action (searching a lost child), and the color of the bird's feather. A comment should be made here about the choice of the first example: when one knows Chinese culture, and the particular strong emphasis made about the relation between parents and children, one can know this particular choice is not an accident. The glorification of the family, the importance of biological longevity through the offspring, the cult of the ancestor, point indeed toward a strong emotional outburst when the child disappears. Let's not forget that Zhuangzi has a more naturalistic and peaceful attitude toward life and death, as we see in the story about the disappearance of his wife. In this sense, there is no "hullabaloo" to be made when the child disappears. Thus, for him, things happen by a sort of internal necessity,

and this necessity is efficient: it is peaceful and harmonious, and if
there is an accident, it is part of the process, a process that we have to
trust. Thus, nothing has to be done to keep the purity of the feather's
color. In this context, we can remind the words of Jesus who tells his
companions worried about practical or survival matter, that God takes
good care of plants and animals, so he will do the same for his beloved
humans. Therefore, no reason to be preoccupied: trust and faith are
the key to happiness, to peace, to salvation. But of course, this efficiency is above our "understandable"and "controlled"efficiency. This
higher order efficiency is an efficiency that denies anything we know
or think about in terms of efficiency.

In the next passage, the author attempts a synthesis of the whole
issue, in relationship to speech and intellectual preoccupation. "The
simplicity of black and white isn't enough to debate over". Which
means that this reality is beyond argumentation, beyond theoretical
speculation: it refers to the "illumination of evidence". Thus, the simplicity of nature is beyond speech: that is why it is efficient, since no
complication is possible; we remain speechless. We should mention
here that the issue of color and form was the object of many circum-
voluted debates among Chinese scholars, academic preoccupations rejected by the Daoist philosophers. On the other extreme, "the spectacle of fame and praise isn't enough to count as great", which means
that the vanity of reputation and praise is not to be spoken about either, but for an opposite reason: it is not worth discussing about it,
not even worth thinking about it; we should just ignore it, since it is
vain and preposterous.

Lastly, in order to conclude this passage in an explicit way, we
read the criticism of most human relations, though a harsh metaphor

explaining why Zhuangzi rejects the "humanistic" perspective, rejects benevolence, rejects family attachment, for its blinding effect upon the mind. "When the spring dries up, the fish dwell together with each other on land, spitting moisture on each other and dampening each other with the froth, but it would be far better for them to forget each other in rivers and lakes."

The author describes how human relations necessarily tend to dwindle and shrivel the living and mental space, since the "spring" most likely "dries up". To understand this metaphor, one has to think how any group of persons, social group or family, as time goes by, tend to become stale, dried up, since it closes upon itself and rejects outside interference and contributions. Relations become established and fixed, behaviors become rigid, a "closed doors" atmosphere sets in. Those prevailing patterns lock up the members of this group in an unhealthy pact, where the Dao is ignored, where freedom is lost. A false sense of unity sets in, that is complacently called "group cohesion" or "family harmony". But when one looks closer at the scene, or scrutinize the "puppet show" beyond its appearance, one easily notices the "big lie", the "blowing the cow", as it is called in the Chinese language. Social or family life is often either a scene of indifference, or the one of a power struggle, if not a civil war.

But in order to hide this "drying out", this fossilizing of personalities and relations, members of the group "spit moisture" on each other. What is this "moisture" and "froth", geared at softening the hardship, and alleviating the pain? It is all the nice speeches, the "selling an image" - our family is the best, the sentimental declaration, the normalized rituals, the reductionist morality, the satisfaction of desire and greed, etc. A speaking image that comes to our mind is the importance given to food, to those "happy meals", where no real discussion takes place, between family members, or friends. Through the pleasure of the mouth and the stomach, the participants try to forget the emptiness of their life, the poverty of their relations, their empty dialogues, the deep tension and resentment that are felt, although denied or suppressed, otherwise the hidden guerilla would break out. How many times have we observed this theatre in our work! Behind the initial official speech about family unity - no problem, everything is fine - are hidden sadness and anger, the feeling of impotence, of lives devoid of meaning and joy! Thus Zhuangzi invites those dejected and miserable persons to open their mind and existence, to widen their space and tread new paths, to escape this deceiving and sorrowful moralizing, and jump in the wide world, in order to have access to the Dao. A more nourishing and more merry perspective than the familial or tribal worldview most human beings get trapped into, where our "little club"becomes the stifling limit of our universe. A much more efficient way to fulfill one's life, a much more efficient way to be happy and free. But of course, one has to give up the "clinging", the fear of loss, the fear of the infinite that prohibits such an existential efficiency.

Benevolence and righteousness

Those puny sentimental and moral intentions interfere with one's spontaneous capacities, they are an obstacle to genuinely adroit action. They are not natural, they are conventional, and in that sense are obstacles for the Dao. Zhuangzi thinks that the ideals of benevolence and righteousness, even though they provide an illusory sense of certitude, are vague and impractical, conceptually self-defeating. In the absolute, caring about everyone is anyhow an obscure, unworkable ideal. It is generally expressed in a very partial, reduced and biased way, depending on each one's subjectivity, which therefore leads to conflicts, since the objects differ and can be opposed. Our preoccupation with "my child"or "my spouse"can easily enter in conflict the "my child"or "my spouse"of the neighbor. As for righteousness, it naturally provokes arguments and fights, since each one's view will easily not correspond to his interlocutor's. Pursuing benevolence and righteousness is wasteful and ineffective, since it results in misdirected effort and needless commotion. And through this misguided effort, devotion to benevolence and righteousness disrupts people's inherent nature. Let us not forget that the Dao is present in the human being, as in everything that exists: it is just that unlike animal who have nothing else, we have all kind of intentions that distract us from this powerful force. That is how, in a practical way, benevolence and righteousness may be self-defeating, estranging us from the Dao. In opposition to "benevolence", Zhuangzi, following Laozi, appeals to natural, spontaneous patterns and tendencies. Instead of fixing benevolence and righteousness as guidelines, we need to only apply our inherent "virtuosity", our "De", through which we can find a spontaneously occurring "way"in any situation, instead of the superfluous inefficient "hustle and bustle". This "De"refers to our personal nature-given potency, power, capacity, or proficiency by which we can follow the Way.

The other way by which benevolence and righteousness are inefficient, is due to the emotional turmoil they engender, since they confusedly torment our hearts, engendering disorder. When following the Way is peaceful, simple and easy. Moral righteousness is a desperate, futile and inadequate response to pathological circumstances. Moral obligations are crutches, and as long as we rely on them, we prevent ourselves from following the Way adeptly. Moral behavior signals loss of or alienation from the Way, disrupting or crippling of our powers of agency, instead of nurturing our health and exercising our innate functioning, in order for our nature to flourish. Paradoxically enough, the Dao de jing says: "Cut off benevolence and castoff righteousness, and the people will return to filial devotion and parental kindness", as if there was an apparent "devotion and kindness", in opposition to a true one. We can explain this by saying that an action that issues directly from virtuosity in response to the Way fulfils the ends of benevolence and righteousness without the agent even intending to do so. From there the criticism of "intention", and the idea of wu wei. Things should happen out of exercising our fundamental virtue, without the obstacles of intention and duties, since the paths of right and wrong are tangled-up and confused. Another angle of criticism, dear to Zhuangzi, is the "forgetting"dimension, the unconscious nature of "true action"that we must reach, as described for example with the cook, the wheelwright or the rooster in different stories. Just like we will forget a perfectly fitting belt or shoe, the action must take place by itself. Therefore, any supplementary attention of emotional attachment becomes a problem, and an obstacle. In a funny way, right action implies a "forgetting the world", just as "people forget each other"and the "world forgets us". The "harmony"becomes then something natural and peaceful, instead of being the object of tension and overzealous attention.

We should specify, if it is not clear, that Zhuangzi does not radically reject benevolence and righteousness. The main problem is what we do with it, how we apply it. One important criticism is that those moral principles were never intended to be absolute or universal norms, but only temporary expedients. They were never more than improvised provisional tools. For "the perfected people of old", benevolence was a "makeshift way" and righteousness "a temporary lodging" from which they went on "to wander in the meandering emptiness", aiming at no particular destination. The right aim is to find what fits the situation, in response to the needs of those involved, without relying on predetermined standards. Since the Way is a process of ongoing transformation, one must "conduct oneself as a person in relation to this process of transformation". Competent conduct rests primarily on an implicit, uncodifiable feel for and responsiveness to one's situation. But Mohist and Ruist thinkers sought to identify the Way with norms that are constant or regular when Daoist texts typically depict the Way as continually shifting and transforming, following no fixed or predetermined boundaries. "Open skills" contrast with "closed skills", in which the action is the same every time. An open skill would be for example "being in balance", which is not a specific posture. It is a relation between the parts of my body and the environment, indicated by how my body feels, determining what I am able to do next. The teacher might still criticize the student for a particular fault in a particular context, his criticism is an effective hint for finding the Way. But in no way should it be mistaken for the Way itself. On the other side, in the Confucian Analects, benevolence and righteousness are central to the life of the gentleman, the text's ethical ideal. He "dwells" in benevolence, never violating it "even for the space of a meal" and adhering to it even in moments of urgency. He would not relinquish it even to save his life. Those values are a universal or fundamental standard by which to evaluate or justify conduct. Daoism focuses not on moral theory, but on morality as a practice, and the right attitude is the morality of the Way. The Daoist critique thus aligns with Nietzsche in rejecting morality as a cultural practice on the grounds of its pernicious effects on human flourishing, for its "anti-life" posture. We should not guide action by deliberately attempting to follow fixed ethical norms. Instead, we are to seek the most responsive, fitting, effective, or harmonious way forward, given our concrete circumstances. We are able to work our way through life situations because of our inherent virtuosity, which amounts to an inborn aptitude for the "arts of the Way", completed with acquiring and developing skills through exercise. We can most effectively guide action directly through this aptitude, rather than through the mediation of moral norms. They reject the idea that justification or evaluation by appeal to these moral values is privileged or authoritative.

Daoist critics generally reject the idea of any stronger, more authoritative justification or evaluation beyond what tentatively seems most fitting. To Daoist writers, it is pointless to claim any stronger justification for such courses of action, beyond the fact that they work, provisionally. Daoist critics of morality may conflate normative with descriptive issues, contending that whatever exists naturally is thereby appropriate or right. They are not advocating immorality or amorality, nor "anything goes". Rather, they are urging more adept performance in applying our capacity for skilled, responsive agency, in order to follow the Way. Their recommendations can sometimes overlap with values affirmed by various conceptions of morality. But the unifying ideal is not moral; it is simply to find, for each particular situation, an appropriate path by which to proceed, applying standards of good fit that may themselves change with circumstances of action open to us. In that sense it is a practical vision more than a theoretical one. And there is no end to the improvement of our behavior. For the Way is no straight and narrow path, something we can commit to in advance and articulate as a definite scheme of distinctions. « Wander in the aimless and wild way, unbound and without inhibition, turning and changing."

Filial piety

Confucianism rests on teaching three essential values: filial piety, humanness or benevolence and ritual, sometimes called ritual consciousness. The Confucian tradition as well lies on the idea of five cardinal relationships, such as a relationship between a ruler and a subject, a parent and a child, a husband and a wife, an older brother and a younger brother, and finally between a friend and a friend. Relationship between a parent and a child that is usually expressed on a concept of filial piety is considered the most important fundament of all, as such relation teaches the value of respect and reciprocity. Confucius considers the latter a principle for the conduct of life: to do to others what you would want the others to do to you. Benevolence then stems as a result of filial piety.

A person endowed with filial piety will not show disrespect to the ones superior to him, will not let them down and will sacrifice himself. Respect is further linked to a state of order: if one is respectful he will never be the one to create disorder or imbalance. Filial piety is the ordering principle without which chaos would dominate. Already at this point the difference with Zhuangzi's message is striking when he writes: "When benevolence and righteousness confusedly torment our hearts, no disorder is greater". Confucius calls order what Zhuangzi names confused torment. Below we will examine the reason for such counter-intuitive judgement.

A character for the Chinese word "filial" is 孝, "xiao", which is composed from two ideograms: an old man sitting on a young child as a sign of support and sacrifice. In China we find very famous stories on the theme called The 24 Filial Exemplars that are a somewhat shocking representation of the importance of this sacrifice in relation to the older generations. These stories were originally written by Guo Jujing in about XIIIth century in Fujian province. Although the idea of filial piety is found long before, even in the pre-Confucian period, for example in the I Ching, the Book of Changes, where the importance of obedience towards the superiors is explained and then later on we find dialogues between Confucius and his student Tseng-Tzu in the texts of Confucius "Classic of Filial Piety", in the Doctrine of the Mean or in the Analects. The concept is very popular not only in China, but throughout the whole Asia, remaining one of the fundament of morality for many years.

Guo Jujing was himself known for his filial piety and then decided to write these 24 stories that mostly depict sons committing deeds of the outmost generosity for their mothers and sometimes fathers. The stories are very short, not elaborate at all, their only purpose is to give a direct, straightforward message to the children. Some of them describe such atrocities as a son cutting off his own leg to feed his mother, a father burying his 3-year-old son in order to leave more food for his mother, a son eating feces of his father in order to determine if he is close to death or not, a son tasting all the medicine of his mother before giving it to her, etc. In such a vision it is considered that the body of a child as well belongs to his or her parents, since he or she is a continuation of their body, therefore sacrificing the body is only natural.

Each story usually ends with appraisal of such behavior, sometimes a little poem that depicts how this behavior was respected and remembered for years after. One of the stories is even called: "The spirit of filial piety moved heaven", to show that a necessary reward will follow. In some stories a grown up son longs for the times when he used to do hard work for the parents, and even though he became wealthy, he wishes that he would return to that hard work, feeling hungry and miserable, simply in order to be with his parents.

There is no reflection offered, no dilemma posed by these texts, only a direct indication at how one should feel and behave; a reader is not supposed to arrive at a conclusion by himself: it is already given to him. It seems that one acquires identity and starts to exist only when one becomes a parent or as a child of his parents. Then one has some meaning, no matter how painful and unbearable it is. Parents should not earn respect or good attitude towards them, they get it by definition, simply because they gave birth. The texts want as well to give an impression that staying with your parents in total fusion and suffering is the greatest and most pleasurable choice one can make. The only purpose of parents'life is to survive: in the stories they are always in the lack, something is always missing, mostly food and health. The sole drive of their existence is then to get a little bit of money in order to eat; when a child helps them to fulfill this drive, they are content. What is even more interesting is that it is mostly a child who feels the great happiness and satisfaction: the more he sacrifices, the more he fulfills his life. This relationship is reciprocal: parents are not supposed to let their children go away and children are not supposed to want it. This is where the phrase "do to others what you want to be done to you"takes a horrific turn and justifies the most savage and barbaric acts. Benevolence then becomes a psychical and mental prison that both parties are meant to enjoy. The part of experiencing joy is crucial in the stories, which means that the absence of joy should lead to guilt. You are supposed to suffer, but you should rejoice while suffering. Even though starting XIXth century such a radical attitude towards filial piety was criticized and even considered an obstacle towards modernization and development, the mental scheme is still very much present in Asian culture, for example through the fear and reluctance to leave their parents or make them leave on their own, something that is considered natural and healthy in Western culture.

Zhuangzi uses an image of the "fishes on the land" to criticize such an attitude: "When the spring dries up, the fishes dwell together with each other on land, spitting moisture on each other and dampening each other with the froth, but it would be far better for them to forget each other in rivers and lakes". Zhuangzi makes an analogy between close relations and those fishes on the land, suffocating and spitting on each other in a desperate attempt to survive, but not even thinking about the possibility of entering a lake and even less of forgetting each other in that lake. It is warm and moist together; a bigger scale is forgotten or was never known. And the one who manages to break away from the common spitting pit will be overridden with eternal guilt and sadness, being forever nostalgic about those days of "togetherness". The only joy that is known with this benevolence is the joy of self-destruction and one can wonder to which extent it is possible to rejoice in those circumstances if only because it goes against our natural instinct of self-preservation. That's why Zhuangzi calls upon disorder in order to trouble benevolence and righteousness: the "order" proposed by the stories reeks of human misery with no access to something greater than yourself and your immediate kin. It is the order of half-dry fishes far away from water; the only reason for their orderly behavior being the fact they are half-dead and have no power in them to move away and rebel, they can only maintain each other in this barely alive state. Slowly they forget that it is possible to be otherwise. Are they benevolent to each other?

We can remind ourselves that the second essential value following the one of filial piety according to Confucius is humanness or benevolence: expressing care and concern for the others. The third one is the ritual. All three values are meant to keep the order, maintain people close to each other, making sure they repeat the same actions that will lead to the same results. Zhuangzi asks in the given text: "Why all this hullabaloo, like one who shoulders and bangs a drum to search for a lost child?". One wants to search for one's child creating noise, instead of forgetting the unnecessary efforts and movements and pay attention to what is already there or instead of finding another way. "The snow goose stays white without a daily bath; the crow stays black without a daily inking": there is no need to do something to the goose or the crow for them to be the way they are. But in each story from the 24 exemplars, things are earned through difficult work, sweat and tears. Benevolence is not a given there, it is not joyous, it is not already there, in the state of things and events, it is empirical and reductionist benevolence in opposition to transcendent and englobing one. Dried up fishes do not see the benevolence of lakes and rivers, the one banging a drum searching for a lost child does not see the benevolence of black and white, the one whose eyes are blinded by the chaff does not see the benevolence of heaven and earth changing places.

We can as well find criticism of filial piety in the modern Chinese society, where there exist different researches executed by psychologists that show correlation between the presence of strong reverence towards one's parents or ancestors and a series of cognitive and psychological difficulties. While it is helpful in keeping family ties and bonds and indeed contributes to installment of order, filial piety leads to a strong orientation towards the past and maintaining the same rigid mental structures and traditions. As a result, this leads to resistance to change and strong dogmatism, which is called by some "cognitive moralism": desire to preserve existing knowledge structures, as representing the "good". People who are prone to cognitive moralism will be reluctant to problematize the established ideas, see things from a more global perspective, they will feel more comfortable in a familiar setting, awkward or worried outside of home. Second common problem is difficulties with emotional intelligence: filial piety leads to suppression of negative thoughts towards one's parents; it is not allowed to disagree with the hierarchical order in a family or reflect on one's feelings of irritation or guilt towards the parents, no matter how arbitrary or abusive they are. This means that if a child does not fit a traditional system, he will have to suppress his views and feelings, which will lead to psychological problems. Third problem is the lack of critical thinking and creativity. Most people who were brought up in an environment where filial piety was a strong value show a lack of active and creative learning skills, they are mostly oriented towards achieving high academic results in order to satisfy their parents, but they do not understand or do not have their own motivation to do so. As a result, they would be less prone using their reason and analysis capacity in order to examine a new situation they encounter, with the consequences of this handicap in their personal, social and professional life.

Comprehension questions

1. Why did Confucius remain silent for three days?

2. Does Confucius have a hard time thinking?

3. Why does Confucius compare Laozi to a dragon?

4. What does Laozi think of benevolence and righteousness?

5. Does Laozi make fun of Confucius?

6. Does Confucius understand Laozi's thought?

7. What is the difference between Confucius and Laozi?

8. Why, when benevolence and righteousness confusedly torment our hearts, is there no greater trouble?

9. What is the main message of Laozi to Confucius?

10. Why do "fishes dwell with each other on land rather than forget each other in rivers and lakes"?

Reflection questions

1. Can benevolence be an obstacle to thinking?

2. Is family a place of confinement?

3. Is the world simple?

4. What is a morality that laughs at morality?

5. Why do human beings tend to complicate things?

6. Why would one prefer suffocating closeness to a freeing distance?

7. Is life benevolent?

8. Do we tend to worry in vain?

9. Why do we resist the order of things?

10. Does man seek reassurance in chaos?

Pearl in the mouth

The Confucians rob graves in accordance with the Odes and ritual. The big Confucian announces to his underlings: "The east grows light! How is the matter proceeding?" The little Confucians say: "We haven't got the grave clothes off him yet but there's a pearl in his mouth! Just as the Ode says: Green, green the grain Growing on grave mound slopes; If in life you gave no alms In death how do you deserve a pearl?" They push back his sidelocks, press down his beard, and then one of them pries into his chin with a little metal gimlet and gently pulls apart the jaws so as not to injure the pearl in his mouth.

The dead and the living

In Chinese culture, dead and living beings maintain a close and dynamic relation. The most revealing aspect of this bond is shown by the ritualistic cult of ancestors. The Chinese ancestor worship, or veneration, also called the Chinese patriarchal religion, is an important aspect of the Chinese traditional religion. It revolves around the ritual celebration of the deified ancestors and tutelary deities of people with the same surname, organized into lineage societies in ancestral shrines. Ancestors, their ghosts, spirits or gods, are considered part of "this world". They are neither supernatural, in the sense of being outside nature, nor transcendent in the sense of being beyond nature. The ancestors are humans who have become godly beings, while keeping their individual identities and blood relations. For this reason, Chinese religion is founded on veneration of ancestors. Ancestors are believed to be a means of connection to the supreme powers, such as Heaven (Tian), as they are considered embodiments or reproducers of the creative order of Heaven. For this reason, Confucian philosophy insists on the principle of paying respect to one's ancestors, giving importance to the idea of filial piety. This traditional patriarchal religion heavily influences the psychology of Chinese people.

But a crucial aspect of this veneration, in spite of its very ritualistic, moral and somewhat sacred aspect, is a very practical one: the fact that after they die the souls of the dead persons will live in another world, and from there they will protect their descendants. It is therefore the family's responsibility to appropriately grieve the dead in order to make sure the souls of the departed rest in peace, and in return they will do something for the livings. Therefore, traditionally, burial practice implied to place numerous funerary objects next to the dead, in proportion to the wealth of each family. They give what they can. Rich families might bury gold, bronze, or pottery, whereas poor families may bury clay products or copper. It was thought that the higher quality was the objects buried with the deceased, the better the lives these deceased would have in the other world.

The fact that precious goods were therefore given to the dead to accompany their afterlife, riches put in their graves, has engendered a phenomenon of grave robbing, as described in the present story, a common occurrence in the history of China. It had different motivations, not always motivated by lucrative preoccupations. For example, people wanted to find spouses for their dead relatives'afterlives, believing that even in death they should have company. In order to make their deads happy, they robbed graves to find women's bodies to place in graves alongside their dead male relatives. Of course, it is now rare to see grave robbing of this kind in today's Chinese society. Nowadays, when grave robbing occurs it is often more likely that the thieves are trying to steal relics to sell for money.

But the relationship to the dead, their graves and their bodies, took some other more recent forms, quite revealing of the status of the deceased through their corpse. An interesting case of the symbolic dimension of the dead body is revealed through a more recent occurrence. During the cultural revolution, in 1966, the Jinggang Shan Red Guard Corps of Beijing Normal University gathered in Tiananmen Square en masse and swore an oath to "Annihilate the Kong Family Business", meaning to destroy the influence and aura of Confucius (Kong Tseu). A whole squad went to Qufu in Shandong province, the home of the Kong family, of which Confucius was the most famous member, where were situated the Kong Temple and the Kong Family Cemetery. Along with students from the Qufu Normal College they established a "Revolutionary Rebel Liaison Station to Annihilate the Kong Family Business". A directive was given which ordered to "hold a mass rally and dig up Confucius". So they proceeded to destroy the National Cultural Relics Stelae previously erected, the Kong Mansion, the Kong family cemetery, and the ancient city of Lu. A team of three hundred local workers were recruited into a "Poor-and-Lower-Middle Peasant Grave Digging Team". Their task was to assist the Red Guard Shock Brigade in smashing stelae and digging up the tomb of Confucius.

Different intellectuals who had participated in the last ceremony to commemorate Confucius held in Qufu in 1962 were brought in from

Shanghai under guard to be denounced in a ritualistic fashion, along with Confucius himself. Following the conclusion of the formal meeting and denunciations, the statue of Confucius in the temple was toppled and then carried through the streets of the town to be vilified. The scholars in attendance were forced into the entourage and denounced for being 'Filial Sons and Virtuous Grandsons Paying Last Respects to Kong". Then the team of gravediggers, armed with picks and shovels, went to the Confucius Cemetery (Kong Lin), a large enclosed area containing graves of Kong clan members. By this time Red Guards were already busy pulling down the stone stelae and commemorative arches positioned along the spirit way leading to the main tomb. Then the leaders of the Red Guards realized that there were seventy graves in the Confucius Cemetery belonging to Confucius himself and his direct descendants, but as well another two thousand graves of Kong clan members. They calculated it would take much more than a few days to dig up all these graves. After some deliberation it was decided that they would dig up only the "First Kongs and the Last Kongs", that is, Confucius as well as sons and grandsons, and the last three generations of Confucius' lineage.

As corpses were pulled out of the coffins - the Kong patriarchs their wives and concubines –took place the confiscation of gold, jewelry and other precious objects that had been interred with the dead. The majority of onlookers expressed delight and shouted with excitement as each precious object was recovered from the graves. The discovery of such plunder elicited such local greed and expectation that, given the general rapacious atmosphere, for the following three months there was something of a grave-robbing mania in the area.

Just like we see in the present story, symbolic value of the deceased is heavily intertwined with practical preoccupation, to the extent that both are hard to distinguish. Although we can, as Zhuangzi seems to imply, conclude that the most substantial aspect of the affair is mainly greed, the ritualistic aspect constituting a mere moral veneer in order to maintain a "good conscience".

Rituals

A ritual generally designates a sequence of activities involving gestures, words and objects, often performed in a determined place, and accomplished according to a set sequence. They are most likely prescribed by the traditions of a community, religious or secular, or by some established authority, institutional, group or individual. Even though those rituals have some "transcendent"function, like salvation, education, unifying, transformation. They are largely defined by formalism, traditionalism, invariance, rule-governance, sacral symbolism, and performance. They are justified as a revelation, as a rational process, through antiquity, or as a psychological necessity. Rituals can be loaded with a heavy spiritual dimension, like church ceremonies, or be quite banal and mundane, such as hand-shaking and daily salutations (Good morning) or expression of gratitude (Thank you). To the outsider, rituals often seem irrational, non-contiguous, superstitious or illogical. And for the insider, the nature of the ritual is indeed often not understood in any profound way: the most common characteristic being its self-imposed nature. It can even be described as pathological, as we see in psychology, where the term ritual is used in a technical sense to designate a repetitive behavior systematically used by a person to neutralize or prevent anxiety; it is a symptom of obsessive or compulsive action, qualified as a mental disorder.

The word itself, ritual, derives from the Latin ritualis, "that which pertains to rite". In the Roman juridical and religious usage, it indicated the "proven way of doing something", "the correct performance", established and justified as a "custom". It has a strong social connotation, as well cosmic or metaphysical, as we emphasized when we look at its Sanskrit origin: ṛtá, which means "visible order": "the lawful and regular order of the normal, and therefore proper, natural and true structure of cosmic, worldly, human and ritual events". In other words, the ritual is the mimetic reproduction of the fundamental principles, divine or material, those transcendent principles defining the fundamental order of reality, the invariant. A status that explains the sacred and untouchable dimension of the rituals. All the gestures and words, recitation of fixed texts, performance of special music, song, dances, processions, manipulation of certain objects, usage of particular dresses, consumption of special food, drink, drugs or other substances, that constitute the rituals that are supposed to reproduce or evoke the underlying universal order. And that is exactly what we find in Chinese culture, where at the heart of all the rituals, as a fundamental principle, we encounter the Dao, the "way that things function". Although numerous rituals refer primarily to social order, such as the cult of ancestors, but it still derives from the same principle.

Ritual often utilizes a rigidly organized set of expressions limited in intonation, syntax, vocabulary, loudness, and fixity of order. In adopting this obligatory style, the ritual speech becomes more about style than content. There is no place in this space for reasoning, for questioning, since there is no real explicit content. Because this formal speech limits what can be said, or how it can be said, it therefore induces some rigid relation to any overt challenge. Thus it tends to makes reform impossible and leaves blatant rejection or revolution as the only feasible alternative. And since ritual tends to support traditional forms of social hierarchy and authority, questioning the assumptions implies to challenge the authorities. Because rituals often appeal to a tradition, they are generally concerned with repeating historical precedents accurately. Another reason for its strong rigid formalism: respect for the past. Of course, the formalism of the ritual can vary, for example the difference between an established church ceremony and the fact of holding a dinner for Christmas, where the second is of course much looser in its procedure. Although sometimes, especially when the ritual pretends to refer to some very ancient, millenary tradition, the chances are that the "reproduction" is an invention built up at some point, a mythification of some particular event, in order to legitimize or sacralize the given ritual.

In order to fulfill its role, the ritual, be it of a religious, social, family or individual nature, needs some type of invariance, like a choreography. It needs the striving for timeless repetition, of words or gestures. A type of mental or bodily discipline, for example in fasting or meditation, adds some strength to the procedure, since it is meant to mold dispositions and moods in each participant, especially when performed in unison by the members of a group. In this sense, the function of the rules is primary what can be called the formalism of the ritual. Those rules impose norms, that regulate individual behavior, they constrain the natural tendencies of the person, or impose themselves on him: they must display some artificial dimension in order to attain to some significance. In a way, the harsher or more sophisticated they are, they more they will be noticeable and meaningful. An important aspect of this formalism is the fact it unifies a group, it makes each one go beyond himself, it implies a struggle with oneself, giving up one's subjectivity in favour of a higher order principle. The principle of sacrifice, in the sense of giving up our own immediate self-interest in favour of a higher order interest or gain is crucial. Therefore, neither pleasure nor utility remain the criteria, the ritual is sacred in itself, as an obligation, without of course excluding the pleasure or utility one can find in it, because of its aesthetic or propitiatory dimension. But it should not be its prime motivation: the obligatory dimension, like in morality, is crucial: its accomplishment should not be questioned nor reasoned.

There are different purposes of rituals. First is "passage", which signifies the transition from one status to another: birth, maturity, marriage, death, joining a group, etc., implying separation, transition and incorporation. They can be a mere formality, a pleasant feast, or involve some difficulty or even ordeal, like coming to adulthood in some primitive cultures. Second is calendrical and commemorative events, to mark a particular period, because of natural or historical events. Those connect a community through relation to time, nature, mythological or epic occurrences. Third are propitiatory events, which imply sacrifice, offering or ceremonies, which establish a relation to sacred or divine entities, by praising, pleasing, or placating those entities, in order to glorify them, ask for forgiveness, blessing, material or spiritual salvation, or obtain from them some type of donation. Fourth are the rites of affliction actions that seek to mitigate spirits inflicting humans with misfortune. This may include spirit divination and consulting oracles, in order to establish causes of the problem, and rituals that heal, purify, exorcise, and protect. The misfortune experienced may be individual or broader issues such as drought or plagues. The rites performed by priests or shamans will identify social or personal disorder as the cause, and make adequate behaviour or restoration of healthy relationships as the cure. Fifth are rites of feasting and fasting, such as carnivals, special diets or lent. In those, a community publicly expresses an adherence to basic, shared religious values. It often involves "cultural performance" or "social drama", which allow the expression of the social stresses inherent to a particular culture, working it out symbolically in a ritual catharsis. It often unifies people, as a way to release social tensions. Lastly are political rituals, used for the establishment and conservation of a power structure. Their purpose of their aesthetic function is to engender support and enthusiasm, and to ground the given power in some transcendent, divine or cosmic order, like saving the motherland or some divine right. But in a simpler way it can simply recall to everyone the importance or majesty of a political structure.

Here are some examples of traditional Chinese rituals. The Worship of Heavenly Bodies: the sun, the moon, planets and stars, and also the earth, which often was in fact a political event: the worship of the emperor, considered as the earthly embodiment of the creator of the universe, Shangdi. The Worship of the goddess Mother Earth, who conferred blessings on human beings. From the earliest times in China it was associated with human sacrifice. It was for this reason roundly criticized by Confucius. Those rituals included the worship of mountains, rivers, the soil god, the millet god, etc. The practice of ancestral worship, which embodied the close linkage of the present to the past, via familial lineage. An ancestral temple was erected to house the deceased during their sojourn to the next world. A mutual bond was established, where the living were helping the deceased in their afterlife, and the latter were in exchange protecting the living. The Worship of Ancient Sages and Masters, like Zhou Gong, the Duke of Zhou, who in far antiquity was renown for his magnanimity. As well the Confucius Ceremony, name given to the ceremony for offering sacrifices to the 'Supreme Sage and Teacher', Confucius. It was treated as an auspicious event, one of the five Rites of Zhou whose purpose was to initiate contact with the gods. The other Rites of Zhou were designed to welcome guests, to honour the military, to offer praise, and to appease evil spirits.

Some other rituals are more daily, primarily social rituals, regulating relations, in particularly in terms of hierarchy, quite precisely established. For example, when a subordinate pays a formal visit to his superior, he must observe obeisance. When two officers meet, they both bow simultaneously, with hands clasped. The subordinate individual stands to the west of the superior individual and pays obeisance first, then the superior individual salutes in reply. When commoners meet, they salute according to age, with the younger saluting first. When an individual is on the eve of a prolonged absence, that individual must pay obeisance four times. In the case of a short absence, the individual bows only once, with hands clasped. Another type of ritual is related to the birth and growth of the child. From the praying for the inception of a child when a woman is not yet pregnant to the time when the baby has reached the age of one full year, many rituals revolve around the theme of a long life. For example the Sanzhao rite, where the child will receive all type of handsels, special initiation gifts expressing a wish for good health and a prosperous life, or the Manyue rite, where the child will have its head shaved. The coming-of-age ritual, the capping rite, is the fact of granting a hat to a young man, a puberty rite which both male and female youths took part in when they began to mature, and was especially prevalent in matriarchal society. It can involve as well the pulling out a tooth, dyeing one's teeth, wearing special clothes, or arranging one's hair into a bun. Then the feast of the Banquet Ritual, where three types of meat are served to guests. The emphasis is on the reciprocity of etiquette rather than on dining although the widespread custom of holding a banquet has done its part to strengthen the festive spirit of the communal dining culture. But the seating order at a banquet, the order of the serving of dishes and the etiquette of proposing a toast are all subject to the requirements of gender, seniority and age in this complex banquet ritual where one prays for blessings and discreetly avoids taboos. A ritual that is quite popular is connected to the "gold paper"usage, as well known as "ghost money"or "hell money". They are sheets of paper burnt as offerings, in order to venerate the deceased on special holidays and ensuring they have a lot of good things in their afterlife and lead a lavish life. Hell Bank Notes serve as the official currency for the afterlife, and are used as a bribe to Yanluo, King of hell, for a shorter stay or to escape punishment. Venerating the ancestors is based on the belief that the spirits of the dead continue to dwell in the natural world and have the power to influence the fortune and fate of the living. Their continued well-being maintains them in a positive disposition towards the living, so they can provide special favours or assistance.

In order to conclude, one can look at rituals as an important way to unify a society, to give some meaning and higher purpose to individuals, through symbolic actions, or simply to establish another mode of communication, more universal since it does not depend on the individual specificity. But rituals can as well be criticized for different reasons. First of all precisely because it involves a denial of the individual subjectivity, repressing its expression. Personal desires and expectations are suppressed, with the frustration this can engender. Second because it annihilates reason, since the foundation of these rituals is either totally arbitrary, or based on some revelation. Therefore, any attempt to reason or discuss its content or foundation is considered irrelevant, disrespectful or even blasphemy. Third, the negation of autonomy and the exercise of free will, which grants some unquestioned power to the authorities in charge of the ritual, or to anyone invoking those rituals and wanting to impose them. Fourth, because they maintain a rather traditional, conservative and even backward cultural environment, for example through encouraging magic and superstitions, resisting any more enlightened perspective, stopping social and individual progress through the fixity of behaviour that it demands from everyone. Confucius and its followers insisted on the importance of those rituals, although they criticized and reformed some of them, especially when it seemed rather barbarian, like those involving human sacrifice. They saw in them a important factor of maintaining unity and order within society. When on the other side Zhuangzi, and a number of other philosophers remained quite sceptical about them, or rather critical. For those critics, it is not so much the ritual that is decisive in the constitution of a good society, but the development of the individual, its capacity of access to the Dao. It is these more fundamental capacities, not their manifestation in a particular system of ritual norms that provide the root explanation of our ability to communicate or to live together harmoniously. Ritual is in a way useful, but normatively justified rituals should be less rigid, less comprehensive, less fastidious, and more spontaneous than traditional culture and Confucianism would allow.

Hypocrisy

"The mouth pearl" story presents to the reader an interesting problem about morality, quite common in human behaviour. It describes a strange combination of righteousness and greed, otherwise a combination of morality and immorality, a phenomenon which can be called moral hypocrisy: the practice of claiming or manifesting moral standards to which one's own behaviour in fact does not conform. Clearly

the graverobbers are first of all pursuing a simple desire to steal something that does not belong to them, but the way they do it, the formalism they apply, seem to endow their action with a certain degree
of morality. Let us examine what are those formalisms and how they
function. First of all, the narration tells us, in an ironical way, that the
Confucians rob graves in accordance with the "Odes and ritual". Of
course, such a conception does not exist, it is a sarcastic invention of
Zhuangzi, since "Odes and rituals", in the style of the great classics
should concern only moral actions. And the desecration of a tomb is a
rather despicable action. But the author quickly warns us that under
the guise of following the tradition, by remaining within the moral
and ritual obligations, wrongful actions can easily be committed. This
refer to the idea that morality and rituals are lower forms of principles,
that can easily ignore superior principles, such as benevolence, De or
Dao. Therefore, under the guise of some formal authority such as the
works of Confucius or other texts of the tradition, one can just pursue
and satisfy his own primitive desire, his own selfishness and greed. A
contradiction that of course can be found within other cultural matri-
ces, as we will describe later on. All is needed to give a varnish of
morality, a form fitting established canons of behaviour, in order to
hide the reality of the action and make it acceptable to the common
eye. In general, a sort of social pact is established, which consists of an
agreement where any critical thinking is banned, in order not to trouble everyone's somber little schemes. And it is precisely this formal
elaboration that constantly Zhuangzi attempts to deconstruct through
numerous narrations.

The announcement of the leader, described as the "big Confucian"
is quite revealing in this aspect. Of course, he is the expert in canon-
ical behaviour, therefore supposedly more knowledgeable and moral
than his underlings, those who are doing the "dirty work". Such a

noble person should not dirty his hands, he just gives instructions, an already important sign of the hypocrisy of the character. The way the story unfolds, he probably stayed outside of the grave, keeping out of actual action, remaining in a distant position. We should here remind the reader of the importance that Zhuangzi attributes to action, to practical activity, in opposition to formal knowledge, which he finds artificial and vain. To underline the hypocrisy of this "learned" person, in order to show to the reader his deceitful behaviour, he shows his fear of daylight. He prefers the darkness, when his mischievous deeds can be accomplished in secret, when no one sees, therefore avoiding truth and shame. As he expresses it, he fears the "light", which will reveal the reality of his actions, he wants to know if the wrongdoing is done, a misdemeanor which he cautiously calls "the matter proceeding", in a formal and neutral way.

The way the little Confucians –the actual perpetrators of the robbery - answer, displays some more of this hypocrisy. They speak as if their undertaking was following an established ritualistic procedure, where the clothes have to be taken off while pronouncing some semblance of sacred words. We should remind the reader that the "Odes" mentioned earlier were classical poetic stances used to accompany some determined rituals, which attributed some ceremonial or sacred dimension to the actions taken. "The grain greening on the grave mound" indeed sounds quite poetic. The following verses have a moral sounding, since it declares that the defunct was not a generous person in his life, he lacked benevolence since he gave no alms, and therefore did not deserve a pearl in his afterlife. The robbing can therefore seem as a just retribution of an immoral behaviour. A totally arbitrary accusation that is used to justify the robbing of the pearl. One should here be reminded that a pearl is a precious object that traditionally symbolizes wealth and power, capturing well the greed that motivates the characters of the story and their real motivation.

Lastly, the description of the extraction of the pearl, he "gently pulls apart the jaws", would as well seem to derive from a quite a gentle and delicate attention, until we learn than the reason for this gentle behaviour is to "not injure the pearl", which of course would then be less valuable. In this case, it is not so much morals that is rendered suspicion, but benevolence, although morals –or righteousness - and benevolence are two concepts that often come together in the Chinese culture. Broadly, 'benevolence'refers to demonstrate kindness or goodwill toward others, being reliably disposed to engage in such conduct. 'Righteousness'refers to what is morally right or appropriate. Early Chinese texts often pair these two cardinal values as a compound, 'benevolence-and-righteousness'(rén yì). They can combine in a broader sense of what we call 'morality'.

In the case of this story, as we can observe in a more general context, in daily life, benevolence, the desire of doing good, the fact of having good intentions, is transformed or showed into a more mischievous, calculating and covetous scheme. In this case, Zhuangzi, as an acute observer of the human mind, speech and motivations, identifies the convenient confusion in which we easily indulge when we pretend to be animated with a good will, when we are well meaning. The action itself is gentle, characterizing the way the man pulls apart the jaws, therefore it looks rather nice. But his motivation is rather petty and cheap. This reminds us of politeness, where one displays polished manners, a behaviour that can be thought respectful or pleasant, but which, actually, is very practical when it is time to avoid a real discussion or say the truth about a situation. In fact, when someone is very nice to us, we become suspicious, we think this person is too nice to be truthful, and this excess of "niceness"is highly suspicious. We can in fact emit the hypothesis that no one is nice without a certain agenda, even if it is simply to be appreciated, liked, of thought well of. Let us remind here the reader that for Zhuangzi, the Dao is the principle we should abide by, and not benevolence or righteousness, which are of a lower order. The main reason is that in opposition to the Dao, they are quite human, therefore mixed with many intentions, consciously or unconsciously. In this fashion, righteousness and benevolence will always necessarily lead to hypocrisy, since it is a lower order reason for action.

The Daoists claim that when Confucius came along he searched for right and wrong, tried to establish it, and in fact caused trouble. He disturbed a naturally harmonious society, engendering greed and desire. When the Dao began to be lost, Confucius began to talk about humanity, rightness, filial piety, which had been practiced earlier on without discussion, but now that they were lost, people started to talk about them, attempting to define fixed principles through language, through speech, trough dogma.

The major criticism against Confucians is that they insist that there is a definable right and wrong. For Daoists, right and wrong are simply a matter of point of view, a matter of taste. Therefore established morality is hypocritical in essence. Confucians, like the rest of us, actually use their egos and try to impose their will. A criticism that resembles a lot Nietzsche's criticism of morality, denounced as a tool to impose the power of a cast upon the majority. Confucians teach some artificial and unnatural behaviour, like ritual and moral education, since they are convinced that they know what they are doing and that everyone should follow them. Their authority is totally unlawful and arbitrary. In the present story, the crooks quote ancient texts to justify themselves and their actions, until they finally manage to steal all the treasures in the coffin. The main point is that concept of ritual and the idea of proper behaviour can be used to legitimize all sorts of bad behaviour in the hands of those with no conscience. One of the axioms of Confucianism is that human beings are social creatures and will naturally tend toward the building of civilization. But the Daoists argue that we have had many civilization and political orders, such as kingships, theocracies, autocracies, democracies, but they all failed at some point. That is because civilization cannot succeed. It is an artificial and unnatural thing. Everything that goes against the Dao is bound to vanish. Civilization cannot be determined a priori. Confucians are therefore wrong on two important accounts: there is no absolute standard of right and wrong, and civilization cannot be fixed, it is doomed by definition.

Morality

If Zhuangzi criticizes the hypocrisy behind the morality, or the utilization of morality, he as well criticizes morality as such, as a lower order and limited principle, that prohibits access to a more fundamental principles, in particular the Dao. One of the harshest passages against morality is found in another story, in a dialogue between Yi'erzi, a pupil of Yao, an ancient sage king exalted in both the Confucianist and Mohist traditions, and Xu You, a Daoist thinker. Yi'erzi said: "Yao told me: "You must devote yourself to benevolence and righteousness while clearly stating what is right and wrong". And Xu You violently answers him: 'Why come to see me? Yao having already tattooed you with benevolence and righteousness and cut off your nose with right and wrong, how will you wander the aimless and wild, unbound and uninhibited, turning and shifting path? ...The blind lacks the means to appreciate the attractiveness of eyes and facial expressions, the sightless lack the means to appreciate the look of richly colored embroidery'. Therefore Xu You, who rather speaks for Zhuangzi, considers it is rather useless to speak to such a person who is under the spell of morality. The words he uses to describe the state of his interlocutor are quite significant, and they should be examined closely. He describes him as a convict, as a very bad person, since he accuses him, like anyone in his condition, of having suffered the severe corporal punishment inflicted upon felons: their face is tattooed with their crime, their nose is amputated, as an indelible, humiliating, visible and painful stigma on the very body of their person. Therefore, morality, no matter how common sensical it is, is not merely a mistake, not merely an inadequate thinking, insufficient or weak, but it mutilates us, it disgraces us, it even shames us. The idea of "clearly stating what is right and wrong"is not only illusory, but appalling.

Xu You explains further: "How will you will wander the aimless and wild, unbound and uninhibited, turning and shifting path?". In other words, when you will be outside of your fixed microcosm, when you will face unbounded reality, you will be lost, you will have no clear goal, you will not know how to behave and what to do. This might seem quite strange, since precisely Yi'erzi said that righteousness "clearly states what is right and wrong". How can we induce from such clarity about judgment the idea that one would be lost in life? It would seem to be quite the contrary, as a logical inference, since the person knows how to clearly judge, and therefore should be able to determine adequately the course of its actions. The explanation is that ethical principles are determined within a given context, in general a given social situation where rules are established, where people are expected to behave in a certain way in order to be recognized and integrated in the group. A typical example is the feeling of estrangement one can undergo when being plunged in a culture where the codes are totally different from the ones we are used to. We then have to reconsider our understanding of people within those new paradigms, and modify accordingly our behaviour. Thus, those who have a "clear idea", rigidly determined in their modalities of thought and action, will definitely feel estranged and lost.

A simple example we could give would be the one of a driver who is used to road circulation being strictly regulated by traffic lights, who suddenly would be caught in a city where traffic lights are either absent, or not really respected. He would undergo a certain panic and not know how to act, ignoring what decision to take at any given moment. He could not judge appropriately the behaviour of other drivers, a necessary appraisal in order to behave accordingly. Another example, of different nature, would be someone who was brought up in a culture where the word given is rather sacred, where one should morally stick to his engagements, moving to a culture where words are only words, where one is easily allowed to shift perspectives, where being tricky is the rule. Such a "fluid"or "unpredictable"environment would be for him rather unbearable, for diverse reasons, psychological, moral and practical. Human relations would for him be rather uncomfortable and even painful. He probably would easily become indignant, an indignation that would seem awkward and even shocking to his interlocutors. And again, he would not know how to behave, since he would not understand the environment.

Daoist writings often employ a specific vocabulary for expressing disapproval of inept or unsuitable conduct, in particular the "moral" perspective: they denigrate it as being 'confused', 'clumsy', or 'blind', for instance. In other words, "moral clarity"is by definition "muddled" . This implies that the point is not to modify morality, not to improve moral principles, not to replace a given morality by another one, but to reject morality itself, as a totally inadequate modality of thought and action. Therefore, morality is not criticized from within, by redefining moral criteria, through some new definition of the "good and bad", but through an actual rejection of the "good and bad". The reason given here is quite typical of Daoist scheme, where the world, more than anything else is chaotic, a world where Hundun reigns, Hundun being described as the mother. Then we can understand the question: "How will you wander the aimless and wild, unbound and uninhibited, turning and shifting path?"If everything changes, if events are unpredictable, established principles will not be of any assistance: on the contrary, they will blind you since you will not perceive the alterations and mutations of the world. And it will paralyze you, since you will not be prepared and fit to react adequately to a shifting reality, since you are stuck with fixed modalities. The same goes with benevolence, which can be thought of as well as a fixed principle. Indeed, there are moments to "be good"or to "do good", but there are as well moments for confrontation and conflict, as animals know in the jungle, as man knows in society. Benevolence can be thought of as well and criticized as a dogmatic and rigid behaviour, determined a priori, unfit for the reality of the world. The standpoint from which morality is criticized can be characterized as twofold: through cognitive and practical criteria, which are supposed to replace moral criteria. Rather than determining fixed modalities of behavior, we must increase our awareness of a moving reality and be ready for different and novel courses of action. Sagacity, practical wisdom, or virtuosity should replace morality.

One could not conclude from this that Zhuangzi refuses to admit any ethical consideration, no more than his criticism of words or any theory imply to stop using language or deny any possibility of knowing. It is rather that he criticizes the attachment one could develop toward words, fixed knowledge or principles, and the rigidity deriving from such an attachment. It rather indicates his attempt to draw a world vision that is more plastic, defined in a more provisional and contextual mode. Behind his moral criticism is an epistemological criticism.

Comprehension questions

1. What does the morality for the Confucians for the story signify?

2. Are Confucians from the story benevolent with the dead person?

3. What does what the Ode say mean?

4. Why do Confucians from the story quote the Odes?

5. Why would a grave robber be a Confucianist?

6. What is strange in these grave robbers?

7. What conclusion can be drawn from this story?

8. What does the pearl in the mouth symbolize?

9. How could stealing the pearl be an act of justice?

10. Why does the Ode speak about the grain growing?

Reflection questions

1. What are the functions of rituals?

2. Are moral laws a mere convention?

3. Does immanent justice exist?

4. Does morality necessarily imply hypocrisy?

5. Should one deserve everything one receives?

6. Is justice arbitrary?

7. Do we always need an alibi to do something wrong?

8. Can morality engender cruelty?

9. Can a person determine what is good and bad for others?

10. Why does greed prefer to hide itself?

Index